ECONOMIC HISTORY

AGRICULTURAL DEPRESSION AND FARM RELIEF IN ENGLAND 1813–1852

AGRICULTURE

AGRICULTURAL DEPRESSION AND FARM RELIEF IN ENGLAND 1813–1852

LEONARD P. ADAMS

LONDON AND NEW YORK

First published in 1932

Published in 2006 by
Routledge
2 Park Square, Milton Park, Abingdon, Oxfordshire OX14 4RN
711 Third Avenue, New York, NY 10017

First issued in paperback 2014

Routledge is an imprint of the Taylor and Francis Group, an informa business

© 1932 Leonard P. Adams

All rights reserved. No part of this book may be reprinted or reproduced or utilized in any form or by any electronic, mechanical, or other means, now known or hereafter invented, including photocopying and recording, or in any information storage or retrieval system, without permission in writing from the publishers.

The publishers have made every effort to contact authors and copyright holders of the works reprinted in the *Economic History* series. This has not been possible in every case, however, and we would welcome correspondence from those individuals or organisations we have been unable to trace.

These reprints are taken from original copies of each book. In many cases the condition of these originals is not perfect. The publisher has gone to great lengths to ensure the quality of these reprints, but wishes to point out that certain characteristics of the original copies will, of necessity, be apparent in reprints thereof.

British Library Cataloguing in Publication Data
A CIP catalogue record for this book
is available from the British Library

Agricultural Depression and Farm Relief in England 1813-1852
ISBN 0-415-38145-2 (volume)
ISBN 0-415-37652-1 (subset)
ISBN 0-415-28619-0 (set)

ISBN13: 978-1-138-86510-5 (pbk)
ISBN13: 978-0-415-38145-1 (hbk)

Routledge Library Editions: Economic History

AGRICULTURAL DEPRESSION AND
FARM RELIEF IN ENGLAND 1813-1852

AGRICULTURAL DEPRESSION
AND
FARM RELIEF IN ENGLAND
1813-1852

LEONARD P. ADAMS

FRANK CASS & CO. LTD.
1965

First published by P. S. King & Son, Ltd.
and now reprinted by kind permission of The Staples Press.

This edition published by
Frank Cass & Co. Ltd., 10 Woburn Walk, London W.C.1.

First edition   1932
New impression 1965

To

J. NELSON NORWOOD

WHO HAS BEEN BOTH
TEACHER AND FRIEND

PREFACE

THIS study, which was completed under the direction of the Department of Economics of Cornell University, was originally intended as a comparative analysis of two agricultural depressions about a century apart. But this project was finally abandoned in favour of a more detailed study of one of them. The depression in English agriculture following the Napoleonic Wars was chosen mainly because of the relative paucity of writing on this notable period in contrast to the wealth of material dealing with the world-wide depression in agriculture following the World War.

It was the striking similarity of the general problems of agriculture and the relief measures proposed in these two periods which first attracted the attention of the writer. Surely, if there is any truth in the old adage, " History repeats itself," it would be worth while to make a more careful and detailed study of the earlier period. In view of the above-mentioned narrowing of the original scope of the study, the task of applying the facts and conclusions to present agricultural problems rests largely with the reader. Whether or not the experiences of the English agriculturists of more than a century ago prove to be useful in analysing present problems, they at least show that neither the current difficulties of the farmers, nor the relief measures proposed, are new.

It is probably superfluous to say that the writer does not aspire to the distinction of having settled conclusively the acrid debates over the cause, or causes, of that century-old agricultural problem. The opinion of that time on these matters was sharply divided and the controversy has been carried on by the historians of English farming. Data, more recently come to light, have served to evaluate the validity of the numerous explanations advanced but, in the writer's opinion, conclusive evidence on some points is yet to be obtained.

Whatever merit this study may have is largely to be attributed to the criticisms and suggestions made by Professors F. A. Pearson, P. T. Homan and R. E. Montgomery, of Cornell University. Professor M. A. Copeland, of the University of Michigan, and Mr. R. R. Enfield, of the Ministry of Agriculture, London, England, also made helpful suggestions during the preparation of the manuscript. Finally, I am indebted to Dr. Norman S. Buchanan, of Colgate University, and Mr. Philip L. Gamble, of Cornell University, for invaluable aid at many points in the work.

LEONARD P. ADAMS.

ITHACA, N.Y.

CONTENTS

CHAP.		PAGE
	INTRODUCTORY	xi
I.	ENGLISH AGRICULTURE DURING THE NAPOLEONIC WARS, 1793–1815 . . .	1
	1. English Farming about 1800. . .	1
	2. The Agricultural Revolution . . .	8
	3. The Protective System	15
	4. Obstructions to Foreign Trade during the Wars	20
	5. The Seasons, 1793–1815 . . .	26
	6. The State of the Currency, 1797–1815 .	27
	7. The General Price Level . . .	29
	8. Agricultural Prices	30
	9. The Effect of High Prices on Farmers and Landlords	31
II.	THE CORN LAW OF 1815	37
	1. Origin of the Agitation for a Change in the Corn Laws	37
	2. The Battle of the Corn Laws . .	47
	3. Resumption of the Battle, 1815 . .	59
III.	AGRICULTURAL DISTRESS, 1815–16. . .	64
	1. The Fall in Agricultural and Non-Agricultural Prices, 1814–16 . . .	65
	2. The Distress of Tenants and Landlords .	69
	3. Legislative Relief, 1816. . . .	79

CONTENTS

CHAP.		PAGE
IV.	Partial Recovery and Further Distress, 1817–22	87
	1. Further Depression in Manufacturing and Agriculture	90
	2. The Agricultural Distress, 1820 . .	97
	3. The Landed Classes again ask for Relief, 1821–22	101
V.	Depression and Recovery, 1822–52 . .	113
	1. Effects of the Fall in Prices on Agriculture	114
	2. Western's Scheme for Relieving the Distress, 1822	118
	3. The Crash of 1825–26	120
	4. Corn Law Revision, 1826–28 . .	122
	5. The Farmers again Petition Parliament	125
	6. Some Observations on the Report of 1833	129
	7. Poor-Law Revision, 1834 . . .	132
	8. The Tithe Commutation Act of 1836 and other Tax Reduction Measures . .	133
	9. Legislative Relief asked for Again. .	135
	10. Preparations for General " High Farming "	136
VI.	Summary and Conclusion	140
	1. Agriculture during the Wars . .	141
	2. The First Years of Depression . .	148
	3. Depression and Recovery, 1819–52 .	155
	4. Farm Relief Programmes . . .	168
	Index	179

INTRODUCTORY

It is common knowledge that the post-war agricultural depression—world-wide in its scope—has stimulated the interest of governments, economists and writers in general in the problems of agriculture, producing an enormous amount of factual information and bringing into acrimonious dispute the question of the cause or causes of the farmer's distress. Referring more specifically to the contemporary American situation, one finds that the analyses, relief proposals, and propagandist movements dealing with the farmer's problems have been myriad. One hears to-day a great deal about the injurious effects on the farmer of such things as tariff barriers, excessive competition among farmers and excessive expansion of acreage the world over, falling prices brought about by monetary disturbances and the subsequent mal-adjustment of expenses to incomes, technical innovations resulting in increased output, the unprogressive nature of farmers, the post-war adjustments in Europe bringing greater production and less demand on the outside world for food, and a great many other factors relating to the economic and political aspects of agricultural problems.

To attempt to classify the many theories purporting to explain the cause or causes of the depression is, perhaps, unwise, for the differences among them frequently lie in emphasis upon the relative importance of the several causal factors rather than in the singling out of some few of these forces for exclusive consideration. The same body of factual information may, therefore, support almost as many explanations as there are interpreters. On this account, the farmer's problems frequently seem to be incapable of any simple and generally acceptable explanation, and in this respect, indeed, contemporary farm problems differ but little from those of the past.

Hence, it is probably unnecessary to point out that this study, dealing with an agricultural depression a century old, was not undertaken with the thought of settling the current controversy over the causes of the farmer's distress. That, indeed, may well be an impossible and fruitless task. It is quite possible, however, that a study of an historical situation similar to the present, even though in particulars the environmental characteristics present marked differences, may furnish a perspective from which current problems may be viewed with greater insight.

Since history affords so many instances of a depressed condition in agriculture, the choice of any one depression for purposes of study and comparison must be somewhat arbitrary. But the distress of the English farmers following the Napoleonic Wars is especially noteworthy because of both its severity and duration. Moreover, many of the conditions, economic forces, and relief proposals in that period of a century ago were very similar to those in the contemporary situation. For these reasons a more comprehensive study of this notable period in the history of English agriculture promised to be both interesting and profitable.

English agriculturists prospered during the Napoleonic Wars, which began in 1793 and ended with the Battle of Waterloo in 1815, just as did farmers in general during the World War. But before the Wars were over prices began to fall, incomes declined, and property values shrank. In the next few years a great many farmers, and businessmen as well, were financially ruined. In spite of the fact that other industries recovered more rapidly, the distressing years of 1815 and 1816 proved to be only the beginning of a long, arduous period for many farmers. In fact, it was not until more than thirty-five years later that those farmers on arable land again experienced boom times, although there were a number of intervening years when they fared moderately well. As might be expected, such a long period of depression brought forth innumerable relief proposals, some few of which were adopted. The farmers relied heavily on help from legislative measures and, as a matter of fact, Parliamentary Committees were frequently appointed to investigate the distressed state of agriculture. But although the farmers' condition was often investigated, little relief came directly from legislation.

Since the post-war problems of the English farmers are to be explained, in part, by the particular characteristics of agriculture at that time and the effects of the Wars on farming, a study of the depression can best begin with a brief résumé of this necessary background. It is with this thought in mind that the first several pages have been written. Subsequent chapters deal with the political and economic phases of the long depression. But a treatment of the strictly economic and political aspects of the farmers' problems is not entirely adequate for a complete understanding of them, since the ideas of the farmers themselves and the opinions of contemporary leaders were among the factors to be taken into account in reaching any successful solution of their difficulties. For this reason, current opinion of those times on many questions has been presented, leaving to the reader in a great many instances the appraisal of its importance. Finally, in summing up the salient developments in each of the periods covered, an attempt has been made to analyse the problems which confronted the English farmers and to estimate the value of the relief measures, both proposed and enacted, in the light of all the available data.

CHAPTER I

ENGLISH AGRICULTURE DURING THE NAPOLEONIC WARS, 1793-1815

THE depression in English agriculture following the long struggle with Napoleon is distinctive because of its severity, duration, and the numerous relief measures suggested. As in the case of any similar economic problem, the difficulties which the landlords and tenants encountered are to be explained, in part, by such environmental factors as the nature, practices, and products of farming at that time. A brief account of the important characteristics of English farming about 1800 and the effects of the Wars on the economic condition of the farmers will aid, therefore, in understanding the nature of the economic forces which turned prosperity into depression in the period following the Peace of Paris.

1. ENGLISH FARMING ABOUT 1800

Towards the end of the eighteenth century, the changes in English life, brought about by the introduction of machinery into the manufacturing industries, were beginning to have a revolutionary effect on agriculture. A growing manufacturing population, no longer in a position to supply its own food, demanded radical changes in agriculture if the country were to continue to be self-sufficient. This was made apparent by the fact that the former balance of grain exports practically disappeared after 1792 and, in its place, a regular balance of imports appeared. This increasing demand for grain explains, in part, the change from grass to arable farming which was taking place. To pave the way for a more complete description of the changes taking place in agriculture, a few facts or estimates concerning the amount of land under cultivation, the uses to which this land was being put and other general characteristics of farming about 1800 may be briefly enumerated.

The Relative Amounts of Pasture and Tillage Lands.

It is impossible to make any accurate statement of the relative amounts of land used at this time for raising stock and growing grain since agricultural statistics of this nature were not collected by any government agency until 1866. Several estimates of the acreage of England and Wales have been made and, although these are probably somewhat inaccurate, they are sufficient for the purpose of this study.[1]

One of the earliest of these was made by Arthur

---

[1] McCulloch, J. R., in his *British Empire*, Vol. I, p. 548, gives a summary of these estimates including those of Young, Couling, Middleton and his own conclusion based on the available information. This is the best source of statistical information on general agricultural conditions in the first half of the nineteenth century that the writer has found.

FARM RELIEF IN ENGLAND, 1813-1852 3

Young, a noted agricultural writer, on the basis of his eastern tour of England, an account of which was published in 1771. He estimated the land under tillage in England at 13,707,000 acres. In 1827, Mr. Couling, a land surveyor, presented a document to an emigration committee in which he gave the arable and pasture land of England and Wales at 28,749,000 acres, 11,143,370 acres of which were tillage lands. Other estimates for this period vary within the range of these two. McCulloch, writing about 1850, came to the conclusion that Young overstated the actual acreage under tillage and that Couling had understated it. In support of his judgment he cites the estimate made by Mr. Middleton, an authority on agricultural matters at the beginning of the century, who placed the amount under cultivation at about 12,000,000 acres. If the acreage added by enclosures between 1800 and 1812 was a net increase to the land under tillage, it is probable that there were about 10,500,000 acres under cultivation in 1800. Even more important as an indication of the condition of farming at that time, however, is a description of the uses made of this arable land.

The Distribution of Tillage Land

Mr. Middleton in 1812 estimated the distribution of cultivated land among the various crops, assuming the total acreage to be 12,000,000, as follows: [1]

[1] McCulloch, *op. cit.*, p. 548.

Table I

Crop.	Acres.	Crop.	Acres.
Wheat	3,300,000	Roots	1,200,000
Oats and Beans	3,000,000	Clover	1,200,000
Barley and Rye	900,000	Fallows	2,400,000
Total			12,000,000 acres.

Importance of Various Crops

This analysis shows wheat to be the most important of English crops and, therefore, fluctuations in its price afford an index of the prosperity of English farmers on arable land. It was grown, at that time, mainly in eight counties in the southeast part of the country on the stiff clay lands. In 1812, it was estimated that an average crop would yield from 20 to 24 bushels per acre.[1] Rye, once important as a bread-grain, was not as extensively used as in the middle of the eighteenth century. This was also true of barley which had come to be used mainly for making beer, porter and British spirits. It was, however, an important crop in the Norfolk system of rotation. Oats were grown in England chiefly for the purpose of feeding horses but in Scotland, where oatmeal instead of wheat bread was the main part of the workingman's diet, it was the most important crop of all. As the rotation of crops became more commonly practised, clover, turnips and beans were more extensively sown. Potatoes at that time were not an important part of the Englishman's diet but they were grown extensively in Ireland.[2]

[1] McCulloch, *op. cit.*, p. 549.
[2] A description of these crops and the counties in which they were grown can be found in McCulloch, J. R., *The British Empire*, Vol. I, pp. 475–6.

Other Agricultural Industries

Dairying and cattle and sheep raising were the other important phases of English agriculture. There seems to be less information available about these for the first part of the nineteenth century than for arable, or tillage farming, but it is safe to say that the growth of manufacturing towns and cities tended to increase the demand for butter, cheese and meat as well as for grain. It frequently happened that all three of these industries were carried on in the same county but it was unusual to find all three on the same farm. The dairying industry, however, tended to associate with breeding and fattening of cattle.[1]

Sheep raising was carried on extensively at the beginning of the century. The number of sheep and lambs in 1800 is estimated to have been 26,148,463, including those in both Ireland and England, and the English production of wool at that time amounted annually to 384,000 packs of 240 pounds each.[2] Although English long wool was supposed to be the best of its kind, exports were prohibited until 1875 in order to prevent foreign competition with the woollen manufacturing industry.

Size of Farms

Arthur Young, in his *Tour Through the Northern Countries in 1769*, estimated the average size of farms to be 287 acres. In 1846, McCulloch considered English farms in general to have varied

[1] McCulloch, *op. cit.*, p. 453.
[2] *Ibid.*, p. 505. This is an estimate by Mr. Luccock.

little from this average. It was true, as he pointed out, that in several instances small farms had been consolidated into large ones but some of the very large Northumbrian farms had been broken up.[1] It would probably not be far wrong to assume that they had not changed greatly in size by 1800 in the light of this evidence.

Relations between Tenant and Landlord

With the break-up of the feudal system of land ownership and tenure, relationships between landlords and tenants became important. The landlord who had probably laid out considerable money in enclosing and improving his estate would naturally be anxious to find tenants who were good farmers and who would improve their holdings. Tenants were anxious to find good farms but they would be unwilling to put much of their own money into them unless they were sure that there would be an opportunity to realize a return on it. The problem, then, was one of finding some form of agreement whereby the rights of both would be protected and production encouraged.

The system of leasing about 1800 was not very satisfactory from the standpoint of these criteria. Several types of lease were in use but few ran for more than fourteen years. In some cases tenants held the land at the " will " of the landlord, meaning that the tenant could be evicted, or the other circumstances of his holding could be changed, at the pleasure of the landlord. But this, fortunately,

[1] McCulloch, *op. cit.*, p. 456.

was not a common form of tenure. In a great many cases tenants held their farms from year to year with the stipulation that either the landlord or the tenant could give notice of a change after six months' time. Some of the landlords in the best farming counties gave leases running from seven to fourteen years with management clauses attached to them. These, in general, made it necessary for tenants to follow certain procedures regarding the rotation of crops, the upkeep of the land and buildings, and the preparation of land devoted to certain crops. But the longest of these leases was considered by the best landlords and farmers as too short a time for farmers to realise adequately on improvements. They set twenty-one years as the proper period for the endurance of a lease.[1]

"Lady-Day," March 25, was the most common time of entry to farms and the first rent payment was usually due six months later. In some of the southern counties of England it was the custom to require the new tenant to pay for the improvements made by the old. This was often not a satisfactory practice from the standpoint of the lessee, for many times he had to pay for work which was poorly done and of no benefit to him.[2]

Agricultural Population

The census of 1801 showed the population of England and Wales to be 8,892,536 and that 2,164,290 lived in the principal cities and towns.

[1] McCulloch, *op. cit.*, p. 462.   [2] *Ibid.*, p. 462.

It would probably be conservative to estimate those directly dependent on the produce of the soil at not less than two-thirds of the total population.[1]

2. The Agricultural Revolution

England, from the close of the seventeenth century until well past the middle of the eighteenth, was a grain exporting country. But after 1765 import balances began to appear and 1792 was the last year of any considerable exports of cereals. Probably one of the most important factors bringing about this change was the revolution in manufacturing industries resulting from the substitution of power-driven machinery for human labour. The rapid growth of manufacturing caused people to migrate to towns and cities and introduced an increase in occupational specialisation.

This one change is not suggested as being sufficient in itself to account for the reversal of trade balances in grain. But it was significant for English farming in that it made a change in the system necessary if the country were to continue to be independent of foreign supplies.

Another important factor affecting the demand for food products was the increasing population. For the period before 1801, it is necessary to rely on estimates for information about its growth, since a census was not taken till the beginning of the nineteenth century. The estimates of Mr. Finlaison of the National Debt Office show that the population of 1750 was little greater than that of 1700, but

[1] McCulloch, pp. 463-4.

there was a rapid increase after 1760.[1] The following table gives the estimates which were based on information from the Population Acts.

TABLE II

POPULATION OF ENGLAND AND WALES FROM 1700 TO 1801 INCLUDING THE ARMY, NAVY AND MERCHANT SEAMEN

Years.	Population.	Years.	Population.	Years.	Population
1700	5,134,516	1740	5,829,705	1780	7,814,827
1710	5,066,337	1750	6,039,684	1790	8,540,738
1720	5,345,351	1760	6,479,730	1801	9,172,980
1730	5,687,993	1770	7,227,586		

This rapid growth of numbers after the middle of the eighteenth century was caused by a declining death rate rather than an increasing birth rate.

While these significant changes were taking place, agriculture appeared to be asleep except for the individual accomplishments of Tull, Bakewell and some few others. The discoveries of Bakewell in the proper breeding of stock were, however, more readily adopted by farmers than were the improvements made in tillage. The counties of Norfolk and Leicestershire were fortunate in having such landowners as Lord Townshend and Mr. Coke and, consequently, these two afforded the best examples of progressive farming at the beginning of the nineteenth century.

Coke owned a large estate in Norfolk, and it is said that his farms commanded competition among the pick of English tenants. He encouraged improvements by granting long leases and the high rents had the effect of stimulating efficiency. " My best

[1] McCulloch, J. R., *The British Empire*, Vol. I, p. 399.

bank," said one of his tenants, "is my land."[1] It is said that this one county exported more wheat from its four ports of Yarmouth, Lynn, Wells and Blakeley than all the other ports of England together.[2]

While these two counties and some five or six others had made some progress, there was evidence, according to Lord Ernle, that other counties had fallen back rather than advanced. Even though some few had achieved success in growing particular crops or breeding cattle and sheep, their methods were not imitated elsewhere. " It will probably be true to say," writes the same authority, " that the country as a whole had made no general advance on the agriculture of the thirteenth century."[3]

Before any great advance could be made in the production of agricultural products, several changes had to be made in the system of farming. Some of the impediments at the beginning of the century were: (1) the prevalence of waste lands; (2) the system of open field farming and common pastures; (3) the lack of proper leases guaranteeing tenants adequate incomes on their capital investments; (4) the poverty and ignorance of the general class of farmers and the obstinancy with which they clung to antiquated practices; and (5) the lack of quick and economical means of transportation and communication.

With the establishment of the Board of Agricul-

---

[1] Quoted in Lord Ernle's *English Farming Past and Present*, p. 220.
[2] *Ibid.*, p. 194.
[3] *Ibid.*, pp. 194–5.

ture in 1793, a movement was started to eliminate these difficulties. The Government did not control this organisation but granted it £3,000 a year to help carry out its programme. Sir John Sinclair, M.P., was made the first president and Arthur Young, who has become famous in English agricultural history for his writings and investigations, was made Secretary-Treasurer.

One of the first objects of the Board was to collect information and, accordingly, commissioners were appointed by the president and sent out to make first-hand observations. Young himself, who is said to have been the soul and inspiration of the progressive movement, made six of these reports before his blindness in 1811 prevented such work. Other activities of the Board for which Young was largely responsible were the establishment of farmer's clubs, and agricultural societies for the exchange of experiences. Ploughing matches were introduced to stimulate competition and live-stock shows were held to encourage better breeding practices.[1]

In 1800 *The Farmer's Magazine*, a journal entirely devoted to agricultural subjects, made its first appearance and rapidly ran through five printings. Another publication was sponsored by the Bath and West of England Society founded in 1777 and the Board of Agriculture supported the *Annals of Agriculture*, edited by Arthur Young, in order to

---

[1] See Curtler, W. H. R., *A Short History of English Agriculture*, p. 229, for a brief account of the establishment of the Board of Agriculture.

disseminate the results of its findings. The enthusiasm for agricultural progress caught even the King in its spirit. George III was proud of his title "Farmer George" and considered himself more indebted to Arthur Young than any other man in the Kingdom.[1]

Young's answer to the problem of increasing the production of farm products was "large farms and large capital."[2]

> "Where [he asked] is the little farmer to be found who will cover his whole farm with marl at the rate of 100 or 150 tons per acre? Who will drain all his land at the expense of £2 or £3 an acre? Who will pay a heavy price for the manure of towns, and convey it 30 miles by land carriage? Who will float his meadows at the expense of £5 per acre? Who, to improve the breed of his sheep, will give 1,000 guineas for the use of a single ram for a single season? Who will send across the kingdom to distant provinces for new implements, and for men to use them? Who will employ and pay men for residing in provinces, where practices are found which they want to introduce into their farms? At the very mention of such exertions, common in England, what mind can be so perversely framed as to imagine for a single moment that such things are to be effected by little farmers?"[3]

Other advantages, such as those accruing from a greater division of labour and full employment of the occupiers of land, demanded the abolition of the small farm.

Young also made war on the old system of open-

---

[1] Lord Ernle, *English Farming Past and Present*, p. 207.
[2] *Ibid.*, pp. 205–6.
[3] Quoted in McCulloch, J. R., *British Empire*, pp. 454–5.

field cultivation and common pastures. The reforms he wished to introduce were intended to remedy the defects of these practices in order that agriculture might better meet the increased demand for farm products. Under the system of open-field cultivation, the strips of land alloted to an individual were too narrow to permit cross-harrowing and cross-ploughing and, for the same reason, it was unprofitable for one farmer to drain his land, or rotate his crops, when his neighbour did not do likewise. The numerous separated strips of land were not economical from the standpoint of the time required for cultivation and they had proven to be a continual source of dispute because boundaries were not definitely set. Since it was the practice to permit the arable lands to be used as common pasture after the harvesting was over, no winter crops could be sown and, at the same time, this system made the scientific breeding of sheep and cattle impossible.[1] It was such conditions which had thwarted agricultural progress, and the great enclosing movement at the beginning of the nineteenth century sponsored by Young and others was expected to remove many of these impediments.

The problem of enclosing these common fields and pastures came to the attention of the House of Commons in 1797. The result was the appointment of a committee to enquire into the state of waste and common lands in the United Kingdom.

[1] See Lord Ernle, *English Farming Past and Present*, Ch. IX, and Prothero, R. E., *Pioneers and Progress of English Agriculture*, pp. 64–6, for a discussion of this system of land ownership and farming.

This committee estimated the amount of waste lands at 7,800,000 acres, 1,200,000 acres of which were under the common fields system and could not be enclosed without the sanction of Parliament. In order to provide for the growing demand for food products, it estimated that:

"Every means should be taken for adding without delay for at least 150,000 to, perhaps, 300,000 acres to land now in cultivation as the only effectual means of preventing that importation of corn, and the disadvantages therefrom, from which this country has already so deeply suffered." [1]

It recommended, therefore, that Parliament pass a measure permitting enclosure in cases where all parties interested had agreed. In other cases, where there was no unanimity of opinion, those who wished to enclose should be given permission. The others could retain their holdings in common.

This committee made a second report which dealt with the expenses of enclosing. A general enclosing bill, it found, would obviate those connected with lawyers' fees in getting a measure passed by Parliament and would, therefore, encourage the break-up of common lands and pastures.[2] Parliament finally did pass a measure embodying these suggestions, but open fields were not specifically dealt with until 1836.[3]

It has been estimated that, in the period 1770 to

[1] Taken from the Report of the Committee which was reprinted in Young's *Annals of Agriculture*, Vol. XXVIII, pp. 512–13.
[2] For the second Report of the Committee see Young's *Annals of Agriculture*, Vol. XXXV, pp. 336 ff.
[3] Lord Ernle, *English Farming Past and Present*, p. 252.

1799, Parliament passed a total of 469 enclosing bills authorising individuals to enclose 858,270 acres. During the ten years 1800–9, a total of 847 bills were passed and 1,550,010 acres came under private ownership. From 1810 to 1819, the totals increased to 853 bills and 1,560,990 acres.[1]

Some progress had been made during the eighteenth century in building roads and something of a mail-coach service had been organised by Palmer in 1784. But the writings of Young and Marshall, as well as the reports to the Board of Agriculture, 1793–1815, show that in most districts much remained to be done. In 1814, Telford was busy making good hard-surfaced roads and a little later McAdam began to compete with him. The result was an opening of new markets for agricultural products.[2]

3. THE PROTECTIVE SYSTEM

At the beginning of the nineteenth century, English industry and commerce were still regulated, to a large extent, by a system of laws constituting the legal manifestation of the system of Mercantilism. Navigation Acts, inaugurated in the reign of Elizabeth, were still operative; wages were still fixed by the justices of the peace in many districts; and manufacturing industries were protected by heavy import duties on competing foreign commodities. This system of government regulation also included

[1] Porter, G. R., *Progress of the Nation*, Vol. I, pp. 156 and 170.
[2] A discussion of highways can be found in Lord Ernle, *English Farming Past and Present*, Ch. XIII. The brief summary given here is taken from pages 284–7.

agricultural products and the most famous of the laws were those governing the import and export of the different kinds of grain, the Corn Laws.

The history of these laws dates from at least the year 1225 in the reign of Henry III. But the first highly protective measure was not passed until 1670. Under this law no grain was admitted free of duty and the import of foreign wheat was practically prohibited when the price in the home market was under 53s. 4d. per quarter by the imposition of the heavy duty of 16s. on each quarter imported.[1] Between the prices of 53s. 4d. and 80s. the duty was 8s., and above 80s. it was lowered to 5s. 4d. Since wheat rarely sold at that time for more than 53s. 4d., the measure was considered highly protective.[2]

In 1689, Parliament gave the farmers even more encouragement by granting a bounty of 5s. per quarter on exports when the price of wheat was at or under 48s.[3] Under the system established by these two laws, England developed a regular export trade in wheat and other grain. Without troubling themselves to show that the laws were alone responsible for the prosperous condition of agriculture during the following hundred years, Parliamen-

[1] The Winchester quarter is equivalent to 8 bushels of wheat and was the standard measure for English grain by 1800. Prices and duties will be given in terms of this measure.
[2] For a summary of the Corn Laws see report of a speech by Mr. Rose, M.P., in Hansard, *Parliamentary Debates*, Vol. 27, pp. 669–80.
[3] Smart, Wm., *Economic Annals of the Nineteenth Century*, p. 90. This work also contains a brief summary of the Corn Laws.

tarians have often referred to the "principle" thus established as one which could not fail to bring about a bounteous and cheap supply of grain for consumers.

The Corn Laws were revised in 1773 and again in 1791, both of the revised measures being less protective than that of 1670. Under the first the heavy duty of 16s. was imposed when the price was at or below 48s.; above this price there was only a nominal duty of 6d. The 5s. bounty on exports was continued when the price was at or below 44s. but when it increased to more than this figure exports were forbidden entirely.[1]

After the passage of this Act, there were a number of years in which imports of grain exceeded exports. During the last two years in which it was in force, farmers received little protection, for the price was continually above 48s. They protested to Parliament and were given higher import prices and duties.

The Act of 1791 raised the import price to 50s. and imposed the heavy duty of 24s. 3d. on all wheat imported under this figure. Above 50s. and under 54s. there was a middle duty of 2s. 6d. which was reduced to 6d. when the price was above 54s. The bounty of 5s. on exports was continued when wheat sold at 44s. or less, but they were prohibited when the price was at or above 46s. Preferential treatment in this law was extended to British colonies putting them on the same basis as was Ireland.

[1] Smart, Wm., *Economic Annals of the Nineteenth Century*, p. 90.

This meant that wheat from these sources could be imported on payment of the regular duties when the home prices were at 48s. and 52s. respectively, instead of at the higher scale of 50s. and 54s. The system of allowing the "warehousing" of foreign grain, begun experimentally in 1773, was continued. This allowed grain to be imported and placed under the King's bond at a charge of 2s. 6d. per quarter. The bonded grain could be sold on payment of the regular duties or it could be re-exported without charge. Such a scheme, it was calculated, provided English shipping with a good deal of business and, perhaps more important still, secured stores of grain which could be drawn on in times of great scarcity.[1] This was the Act in force when the Napoleonic Wars began in 1793.[2]

The Act of 1791, however, afforded little protection to the farmer during its existence. Protection was quite unnecessary after 1793, for the price of wheat kept well above 50s. most of the time until the struggle with Napoleon was nearly over. In the place of the export balance during the early years of the century, one on the import side regularly appeared except for the year 1808 when a large

[1] The summary of this law is taken from Smart, Wm., *Economic Annals*, pp. 91–2.
[2] The export and import prices were determined from averages made up in the twelve maritime districts of England by government officers. The averages for imports were adjusted four times a year; those for exports were determined weekly. Each district had its own regulative prices. Consequently, when one port of the country was exporting another port might be importing grain.
Galpin, W. F., *The Grain Supply of England during the Napoleonic Period*, pp. 2 and 3.

amount of grain was sent to the British troops on the Spanish peninsula. The export of grain was almost continually suspended for the period of the Wars. Instead of granting a bounty on exports, as much as 16s. and 20s. per quarter were paid for imports by the Government in 1795–6 and again in 1800. In these years of famine, neutral ships carrying grain were seized and brought into English ports and Parliament frequently forbade the use of wheat for making starch and whisky.[1]

Following a succession of good harvests, the price of wheat fell to about 50s. in 1804 from the high price of 156s. 2d. in March 1801. This decline was enough, according to the petitions sent to Parliament, to cause the farmers considerable difficulty should it continue. The House of Commons appointed a committee to investigate the situation and to bring in recommendations as to whether any change should be made in the Corn Laws. This committee found that the price of grain, although it had been irregular since the Wars began, had afforded the farmer a "fair profit." But some relatively high cost lands had been brought under cultivation, it said, and, in order to insure the continued tillage of these, the import prices should be revised upward.

Parliament accordingly passed a bill fixing the heavy duty of 24s. 3d. on wheat when the price was at or below 63s. The middle duty of 2s. 6d. was to be paid when the price was between 63s. and 66s. and the nominal charge of 6d. was fixed on imports when the price was above 66s. The bounty on

[1] Lord Ernle, *English Farming Past and Present*, p. 265.

exports was continued when the price was under 48s. and no grain could be shipped out of the country when the price rose above 54s.

The committee further recommended changing the method of fixing the prices regulating imports and exports. It suggested that the prices in the twelve maritime districts be averaged and that this average be used in determining the import and export trade for the whole country. This proposal, as well as the other recommendations, was incorporated in the bill subsequently passed by Parliament.[1]

This law, however, was a dead letter during practically all of the remainder of the war period, since the price of wheat remained, for the most part, above 63s. It was of some aid to the farmers, nevertheless, when prices fell in 1814 and 1815.[2]

4. Obstructions to Foreign Trade during the Wars

Some of the forces bearing on agricultural prices have already been considered in the discussions of the growth of population and its distribution between the country and towns. On the supply side, the progressive movement making for better use of

---

[1] A brief account of the discussion on this law along with its provisions is given in Smart, Wm., *Economic Annals*, pp. 90–7.

[2] It will be noted that only the prices and duties on wheat have been given for the several Corn Laws discussed. This is the usual practice followed by the historians of English agriculture and seems justified because wheat was the most important of the grain crops. The duties and prices on other grains were nearly always changed in proportion to the alteration made in those for wheat.

the land already in cultivation, and the enclosure of common lands and fields, both tended to increase production. The other important factors affecting agricultural prices during the Wars were: (1) the obstructions to trade arising from war activities; (2) the effect of the seasons; and (3) the alterations made in the currency of the country. A brief discussion of each of these factors will help to explain why English farming made great progress in this period.

Foreign Trade Relations of England, 1793-1815

Once England had come to depend on foreign supplies of grain, any obstruction to shipping which affected the grain trade was of considerable importance to both farmers and consumers. During the Wars, each of the belligerents made a pretence of trying to cripple the foreign trade of the other. The " paper blockades " of this period are well known to all students of history. But, although effective enforcement of the many decrees issued by both countries was often lacking, they created hazards sufficient to increase the costs of shipping and, therefore, the prices of all imported goods, including grain. This was undoubtedly a favourable circumstance for the English farmer.

The most important sources of foreign grain supplies were Prussia, Russia, Holland, France and the United States. Prussia, during most of the war period, was the most important single source. The difficulty of access to the Russian ports of Riga and St. Petersburg on account of weather conditions prevented England from relying strongly on this source. France ordinarily grew little more grain than she needed and, except for the years 1809–10, not much French grain was imported. Holland, in spite of the efforts of Napoleon to close her ports, shipped a good deal of grain to England. She furnished more wheat in the famine years of 1800–2 than the combined shipments from Ireland, France, Norway and Denmark, and she continually exported more rye to England than any other one country.[1]

At the outset of the Wars, Parliament passed a measure which prohibited,

"the selling, supplying, contracting for or delivering, on the part of anyone in Great Britain, of military stores, commercial paper or specie of England, forage, foodstuffs, raw and unfinished articles of clothing, to or for the use of the French Government or places annexed to or under the influence of France, its armed forces or agents."[2]

At the same time, however, provision was made whereby persons might carry on a trade with France providing they obtained a licence from the Crown. During the years of scarcity, this licenced trade became an important means of securing wheat in exchange for manufactured goods.

The Act of 1793 was suspended after the Peace of Amiens in 1802. But in 1803 hostilities were resumed and it was re-enacted along with the

[1] Galpin, W. F., *The Grain Supply of England during the Napoleonic Period*, p. 134. This is by far the most complete source of information on this particular subject.
[2] *Ibid.*, p. 84.

same provision for the issuance of special licences. With some slight modifications made in 1809, this measure remained in force for the balance of the Wars.[1]

The Continental System

Before 1806, Napoleon succeeded in closing only the ports of France to English trade. He was less successful in preventing the Dutch from exporting grain to English markets. After the famous battles of Jena and Auerstadt, Prussia came under his control and the Berlin Decree, proclaiming a blockade of the British Isles, was issued.[2] It prohibited all commerce between Great Britain and France, including the States dependent on her. The effects of this decree are shown by the fact that the exports of grain from Prussia declined from 559,628 quarters in 1805 to only 51,523 quarters in 1806.[3]

This comparatively small import from Prussia in 1806 caused no great concern to the country because of the favourable harvest and the ready access to other foreign grain. In 1807, Napoleon's Milan Decree was issued and Parliament responded with more "Orders in Council" until neutral trade with France, her possessions and allies was theoretically entirely prohibited. Partly on account of the poor harvest and, due somewhat to these decrees, not a single bushel of grain was imported from Prussia in

[1] Galpin, W. F., *The Grain Supply of England during the Napoleonic Period*, pp. 89–92.
[2] Cross, A. L., *A Short History of England and Greater Britain*, pp. 602–3.
[3] Galpin, W. F., *op. cit.*, p. 43.

1808. Enforcement of the Milan Decree also cut off the supply of grain from Holland to a large extent between the years 1808–11.

In 1809 and 1810, both France and England were confronted with domestic economic problems which necessitated changes in trade policies. British consumers were faced with a shortage of wheat which had already been selling at famine prices. In France, the abundant harvests in these two years reversed the situation and Napoleon was confronted with a disgruntled peasantry. Prices of wheat were high in England and low in France, a situation which made the restrictions on trade doubly hard to enforce. The result was that both nations decided to permit the resumption of trade for a brief period of time.

For one month, beginning September 28, 1809, the English Government agreed to grant licences permitting the import of grain and flour from the ports of France and Holland. Imports could be paid for by exports of British manufactured goods and colonial produce. Napoleon, however, would accept only bullion and specie in payment for some of the grain.[1] The total imports of grain from France in these two years amounted to 251,498 quarters; those from Holland and Flanders combined amounted to 4,028,319 quarters.[2]

After 1810, the imports from practically all the continental surplus areas declined and neither Flanders nor Holland exported any wheat until

---

[1] Galpin, W. F., *op. cit.*, pp. 111 and 192.
[2] *Ibid.*, Appendices, pp. 243–5 and 256.

1814.[1] But after Napoleon's disastrous winter campaign in Russia in 1812, her ports were opened. In the following year, Germany broke away from his control and, by the end of 1813, the blockade of England had lost practically all of its effectiveness. As Napoleon's system weakened, Parliament withdrew its "Orders in Council" and other restrictive measures.[2]

The decrees had had the effect of making it more difficult to trade even though they had not succeeded in shutting it off entirely. An idea of the added expense to which dealers in foreign products were subjected is given by a table from Tooke.[3]

TABLE III

A Comparison of the Average Freight and Insurance Rates on Baltic Products brought to London in 1809–12 with the Charges on the Same Goods in 1837

Product.	Unit.	1809–12. £ s. d.	1837. £ s. d.
Hemp	per ton	30 0 0	2 10 0
Tallow	per ton	20 0 0	1 10 0
Wheat	per quarter	2 10 0	0 4 6
Timber	per load	10 0 0	1 0 0

Trade Relations with the United States

England obtained some, but not a great deal, of its grain from the United States during the Wars. In the famine years of 1801, 1807 and 1809, the imports from this source were important and more might have come in had it not been for the disturbed

---

[1] Galpin, W. F., *Appendices*, pp. 243–5.
[2] *Ibid.*, see Chapter X.
[3] Tooke, Thomas, *History of Prices*, Vol. I, p. 309.

political relationships between the two countries.[1] England's "Orders of Council" of 1807 authorising British men-of-war to stop neutral vessels which might be sailing for French ports angered Americans. In the same year, Congress passed the Embargo Act prohibiting all trade with European countries. This restriction was fully as harmful to the Americans as to those at whom it was aimed, and in 1809 the *Non-Intercourse Act* was passed which applied only to Great Britain, France and their dependencies. The United States finally declared war on England in 1812 and, consequently, little legitimate trade was carried on between them until peace was established in 1814.[2]

5. The Seasons, 1793–1815

Since some writers have attached considerable importance to the prevalence of poor harvests during the Wars as an explanation of the rise in prices of grain, it will be worth while to examine the size of the crops in the light of the available data. The dearth of statistical data makes it impossible to know definitely what the actual size of the crops was, but the following comparison throws some light on their relative magnitude.

It is said that, out of the twenty-two years, the crops of fourteen were deficient; in seven, namely, 1795, 1799, 1800, 1809, 1810, 1811 and 1812, they failed to a remarkable extent; six produced an

---

[1] Galpin, W. F., *op. cit.*, Appendix No. 8, p. 249.
[2] Cross, A. L., *A Short History of England and Greater Britain*, pp. 608–9.

FARM RELIEF IN ENGLAND, 1813-1852   27

average yield; only two, 1796 and 1813, were years of abundance.¹ According to this statement, the period was remarkable for the number of poor and inadequate harvests. The fluctuating supplies made grain prices erratic and subject to wide variations.

6. THE STATE OF THE CURRENCY, 1797-1815

Of all the factors tending to increase prices of goods in general during the Wars, the alterations in the volume of currency and credit were undoubtedly the most important. From 1797 to 1821 England was on an inconvertible paper basis by reason of the suspension of specie payments by the Bank of England. At the same time, the number of country banks with note issue powers increased rapidly and the result was a state of inflated prices.

This suspension was forced on the directors as the result of large foreign loans made by the Government with money borrowed from the Bank. Rumours of a declining stock of bullion and specie and the fear of an invasion by Napoleon also caused the Bank to lose cash. The directors appealed to the Ministry and the result was a temporary order of Council and, finally, the passage of the Bank Restriction Act authorising the suspension of specie payments. By the provisions of this measure Bank of England notes were made legal tender.

The Act was originally intended only as a temporary expedient but it was continued until 1819.

---

¹ This summary is taken from Lord Ernle, *English Farming Past and Present*, p. 269. For a detailed, year-by-year examination of prices during this period see Tooke, T., *History of Prices*, Vol. I.

28 AGRICULTURAL DEPRESSION AND

An examination of the accounts of the Bank, made by a committee of the House of Commons shortly after the suspension, showed the organisation to be in a strong financial position. It is probable, according to Turner, that the suspension of cash payments was continued for political reasons and not because the Bank was unable to pay its notes in cash.[1]

The Growth of Country Banks

There is no accurate record of the number of country banks in England before 1808. It has been estimated, however, that there were about 200 of them doing business just before the crisis of 1797. After 1808 country bankers were required to procure a licence from the Government and there is, consequently, definite information as to their number, although the amount of their notes outstanding at any one time can only be estimated. Seven hundred and two licences were issued in 1809 and the number increased year by year until in 1814 they totalled 940. Assuming the estimate for 1797 to be at least a close approximation, it can be said that the number had more than quintupled by the end of the Wars.[2]

The notes of these banks were mainly for one, two or five pounds and were usually in active circulation until returned to the source of emittance. This part of the currency is considered by Double-

---

[1] Turner, B. B., *Chronicles of the Bank of England*, p. 90. An account of the events leading to the suspension and the subsequent legislation is given in the same source, pages 77–96.

[2] Doubleday, Thomas, *Financial History of England*, pp. 234–5.

day to have tripled as a result of the rapid increase in the number of banks.[1] After 1806 country bankers were required to pay a tax on the notes which they emitted and the relative fluctuations in this part of the currency can be seen from these records.

7. THE GENERAL PRICE LEVEL

Two statistical studies of the movement of the general wholesale level of prices during the latter part of the eighteenth and the first half of the nineteenth centuries sum up the effect of the factors which have been briefly examined and are here presented in graphic form.[2]

CHART I

ANNUAL INDICES OF COMMODITY PRICES 1790–1850
(a) All commodities (35) (Base: 1790 = 100).
(b) Jevons' indices (about 40) (Base: 1790 = 100).

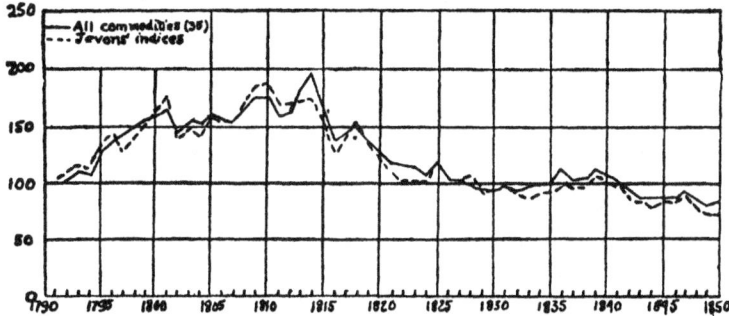

[1] Doubleday, Thomas, *Financial History of England*, p. 235.
[2] Taken from Silberling, N. J., "British Prices and Business Cycles," published in *The Review of Economic Statistics-Supplement*, Preliminary Vol. V, 1923, p. 234. The results of his other studies and a discussion of the methods used are given in pages

8. AGRICULTURAL PRICES

Whenever the general wholesale prices reached their highest point, there seems to be no question that agricultural prices were highest in 1812 and 1813. The following charts of Jevons show the movements of grain and meat prices during the Wars and in the following period of depression.[1] It will be noticed that, although there is a distinct trend, the seasonal variations which have been briefly discussed caused a great deal of fluctuation from year to year.

It can be seen from the charts on page 31 that the prices of both grain and meat more than doubled during the twenty-two years of war. Meat prices rose steadily, with the exception of two minor

---

223–61. He has changed the base of Jevons' indices to make them comparable with his own.

Jevons discusses his methods and findings in *Investigations in Currency and Finance*, 1884, pp. 119 ff., and in the *Journal Royal Statistical Society*, June, 1865.

It will be noticed that the two indices do not agree as to the peak year of prices during the Wars. Jevons' indices show it to be 1810, but Silberling's reached the highest point in 1814. This discrepancy is probably due to the choice of commodities and the fact that Silberling's is an unweighted index while Jevons' contains an element of " haphazard weighting." It has been impossible to compare the actual prices of the different commodities used in these indices, for, although Jevons took his data from Tooke's *History of Prices* which is available, Silberling based his study on prices taken from various sources only to be found in various London libraries. The fact that Jevons' indices show prices in gold instead of currency may also have something to do with the problem.

These indices show that wholesale prices nearly doubled during the Wars and fell off abruptly in 1815 and 1816. After a slight recovery in 1817 and 1818, they continued downward, with the exception of 1825, until 1835.

[1] Jevons, W. Stanley, "On the Variation of Prices," Appendix, p 2. *Journal Royal Statistical Society*, Vol. XXVIII, June 1865.

recessions, to a high point in about 1813. The prices of grain fluctuated a great deal more and show a peak in 1812.

CHART 2

THE PRICES OF CORN (ALL GRAINS) 1780–1860
(Base: 1782 = 100)

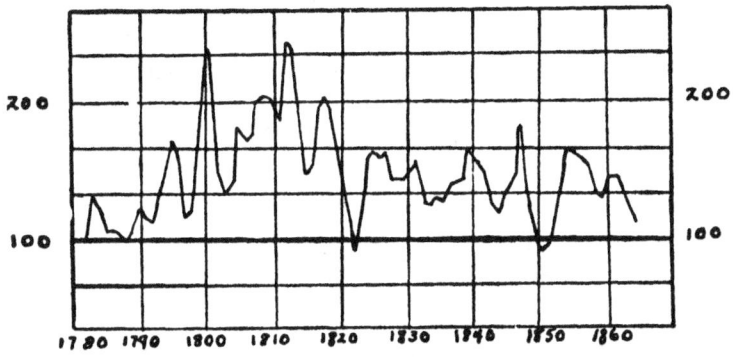

CHART 3

PRICES OF MEAT, 1780–1860
(Base: 1782 = 100)

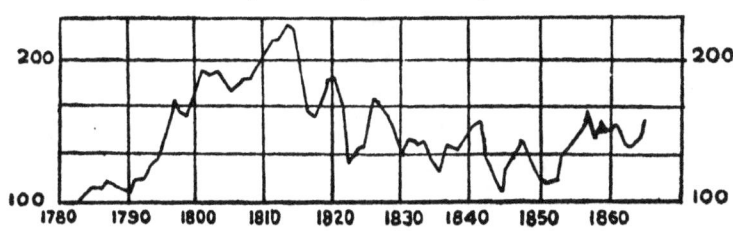

9. EFFECT OF HIGH PRICES ON FARMERS AND LANDLORDS

Rising prices had the effect of bringing about a great many of the reforms urged by Arthur Young in his crusade for the introduction of new methods and practices. As has already been pointed out, a great deal of common-land was brought under private control after 1800 ; pastures were ploughed up ; a good deal of waste land was reclaimed ; and buildings were improved. Some of these betterments were made out of savings and current income but a large amount of the money sunk in land and equipment was borrowed from the country banks. As long as prices continued to rise, there seemed to be no better investment available.

Competition for farms among farmers forced up rents to new heights. In the county of Essex farms could be pointed out which had let, just before the Wars, at less than 10s. an acre; in 1812 they brought from 45s. to 50s. In both Berkshire and Wiltshire there were farms which in 1790 had been let at 14s. per acre and in 1810 brought the landlord 70s., an increase of 500 per cent. In Staffordshire, Norfolk, Suffolk and Warwickshire the rise was about equally as great.[1]

These high rents encouraged landlords to raise their standard of living. Lands and buildings were burdened with mortgages to acquire more property. The same thing was true of the farmers, for, although rents rose rapidly, profits increased even faster. Country mansions were built, re-built, or enlarged, and farmers and their wives adopted more expensive ways of living. The whole fabric rested on the continuance of war prices, although they did not seem to realise it.

[1] Porter, G. R., *Progress of the Nation*, Vol. I, pp. 164-5.

FARM RELIEF IN ENGLAND, 1813–1852

In 1771, Arthur Young made his Northern Tour and estimated the total rental of England and Wales at sixteen millions. Allowing for the depreciation of the currency, McCulloch calculated the increase since 1800 on the basis of the property tax. His estimates are:

Year.	Rent in £.	Year.	Rent in £.
1800	22,500,000	1810	29,503,074
1806	25,908,207	1815	34,230,462

They show an increase in the total amount of approximately 50 per cent. between 1800 and 1815 and the total in 1815 amounts to about 113 per cent. rise compared with Young's estimate for 1771.[1]

The Increase in Expense

It must not be supposed that this rise in prices was a pure gain for farmers and landlords. The expense of carrying on twenty-two years of war necessitated increased taxation. The general property tax, bearing heaviest on the landed classes, was imposed and the various excise duties, stamp fees, and postages on letters were increased to help balance the budget. The revenue from the latter amounted to £33,081,821 in 1801 but by 1814 it had increased to £70,103,344. At the same time, the Government expenditures for the Army, Navy and Ordinance rose from £37,216,268 to £106,832,260, the latter amount including interest on the public debt.[2] In addition to these expenses, England loaned a

---

[1] Young's estimate can be found along with McCulloch's in the latter's *British Empire*, Vol. I, p. 557.
[2] Porter, G. R., *Progress of the Nation*, Vol. II, p. 321.

total of £46,289,459 to her allies. The revenue from taxes and duties proved inadequate to meet these large expenditures and, consequently, the public debt grew from £261,735,059 in 1792 to £885,186,323 by 1815.[1]

Local taxes also increased. At the beginning of the nineteenth century, the sums expended for the care of the parish poor were the largest part of the local expenditures. Justices of the peace since the reign of Elizabeth had supervised the care of the parish poor and in 1795 they inaugurated the practice of supplementing wages out of the poor fund. The burden of making these payments thus fell largely on the property owners and tenants of the parish.

"The farmers [according to one writer] had only to meet together when wheat was 100s. per quarter and meat by the carcase was 7½d. per pound, it having been less than half the price twenty years before, and agree that they would pay their workmen a shilling a day, with the rider that the rest of the public should pay him another shilling which they took care to assess, collect and distribute at their discretion."[2]

Partly because of the maladministration of the poor laws but also as a result of the enclosure of common lands and fields, the sums expended for poor relief continued to increase throughout the Wars. They averaged £2,167,148 for the three years 1783-4-5 and rose to £8,511,863 in 1813-14.[3]

The following table affords a comparison of the

---

[1] Lord Ernle, *English Farming Past and Present*, p. 316.
[2] Rogers, J. E. T., *Six Centuries of Work and Wages*, Vol. II, p. 501.
[3] Porter, G. R., *Progress of the Nation*, Vol. II, p. 357.

farmer's pre-war expenses with those during the years of highest prices. The data were collected by the Board of Agriculture from circular letters sent out to landlords and tenants.[1]

TABLE IV

EXPENSES OF CULTIVATING 100 ACRES OF ARABLE LAND IN 1790, 1803 AND 1813

Expense.	1790. £ s. d.	1803. £ s. d.	1813. £ s. d.
Rent	88 6 3¼	121 2 7¼	161 12 7¾
Tithe	20 14 1¾	26 3 0¼	38 17 3¼
Poor Rates	17 13 10	31 7 7¾	38 19 2¾
Wear and Tear	15 13 5¼	22 11 10¼	31 2 10¾
Labour	85 5 4¾	118 0 4	161 12 11¼
Seed	46 4 10¼	49 2 7	98 17 10
Manure	48 0 3	68 6 2	37 7 0¼
Team	67 4 10	80 8 0¼	134 19 8¼
Interest	22 11 11½	30 3 8¾	50 5 6
Taxes	—	—	18 1 4
Total	£411 15 11¾	£547 10 11½	£771 16 4½

If these figures are representative, it would seem that the farmer's expenses did not quite double during the Wars. In all probability some of them did not increase as rapidly as did the prices of agricultural produce.

The brief summary of the condition of agriculture which has been given indicates that the English farmers were unusually prosperous during the Wars. It is somewhat surprising, therefore, to find certain representatives of the landed classes asking for a

[1] Taken from the Report of the Select Committee of the House of Commons appointed to hear petitions on the Corn Laws, *House of Commons Sessional Papers*, 1814–15, Report V, Appendix, pp. 64–5.

change in the Corn Laws early in 1813 before any signs of depression had appeared. Relatively little progress toward revision of the protective measures was made, however, until landlords and tenants were faced with the ruinous effects of falling prices in the following year. At the same time, the opposition of the manufacturing classes to any upward revision of the duties increased. An account of the ensuing struggle, which occupied a good part of the parliamentary sessions of 1814 and 1815, is given in the following chapter.

CHAPTER II

THE CORN LAW OF 1815

1. Origin of the Agitation for a Change in the Corn Laws

ENGLISH politics at the beginning of the nineteenth century was still largely under the control of the wealthy landlords. Neither the rising class of industrialists nor the common labourer had a strong influence in Parliament. True, there were two opposing political parties. Of these, the Whigs were more inclined to give the manufacturing classes some measure of political power; but they were too strongly " landed " to proceed far in this direction. That " Corn was King " in British politics was well recognised. Fundamentally, however, the Industrial Revolution was creating a sharp divergence of interests which was clearly brought to light in the debates on the Corn Law of 1815.

The landed classes for over a century had used their political strength to protect English farming from foreign competition. Measures providing for both high import duties on foreign grain and a bounty on exports, when domestic prices were below a certain level, had been secured. It was true that the Corn Laws had little effect on prices of grain during the Wars. The other factors which have been briefly examined insured high prices for the farmers without the aid of protection. Both the import duties and the export bounty were practically suspended by the mounting prices of grain after 1804. Before the end of the Wars was in sight, however, a movement was set on foot in Parliament for the purpose of maintaining the war-time level of agricultural prices. This seemingly premature action calls for some explanation.

It was true that the Corn Law of 1804 had been made practically a dead letter by subsequent events. Some sections of this law, however, were particularly distasteful to a particular section of Great Britain. The difficulty was to be found in the clause prohibiting exports of wheat when the price was over 54s. per quarter, and the objectors were the landlords and grain dealers of Ireland.

The high prices of wheat had given Irish farmers an incentive to extend their cultivated areas and plant more and more of this grain. In 1806, the restrictions on Irish imports were removed putting England and Ireland on a free trade basis. This served as an added stimulus. Ireland began to send larger shipments to English markets and, in return, took English manufactured goods. The profitableness of growing wheat depended on the prices in this neighbouring market, and although prices in England were high, they might possibly be higher elsewhere. In such an event, the Irish farmers were prohibited from making the most of the situation by the existing law. This proved to be their original bone of contention but, after prices began to fall in the latter part of 1813, the farmers and landlords of the United Kingdom joined in demanding more protection.

The Irish landlords without much opposition secured the appointment of a Select Committee of the House of Commons in March 1813, instructed to "enquire into the corn trade of Ireland."[1] Sir Henry Parnell, an Irish landlord, was made its chairman. Later an amendment was passed substituting "United Kingdom" for "Ireland" and the membership of the Committee was increased to twenty-seven.

The Committee sat some three or four days and examined five witnesses all of whom were connected with the Irish grain trade. Parnell, himself, was subsequently compelled to apologise for this inadequate treatment of the problem. He pointed out to the House that:

"When the Committee was first appointed, its only object was to examine the Corn Laws of Ireland; and, when it was afterwards suddenly proposed to extend its investigations to the Corn Laws of the Country, those members who were added to it were, perhaps, selected without due consideration."[2]

Prior to the appointment of this Committee, Parliament passed a Bill calling for a return on the quantity of grain imports and exports of Great

---

[1] Smart, Wm., *Economic Annals of the Nineteenth Century*, p. 373.
[2] *Ibid., op. cit.*, p. 373.

Britain from 1792 to 1811 inclusive. This statement was appended to the Committee's report which was presented to the House of Commons on May 11, 1813. The following brief summary of the report shows how ingeniously this data on imports and exports was used.[1]

The return for imports, according to the Committee, showed that the value of foreign grain brought into Great Britain, during the period 1792–1811, amounted to £58,634,135 and that £2,826,947 had been paid as bounties for foreign grain in the period 1796–1803. The average price of a quarter of wheat for the whole time covered in the survey was 77s. 3d.; in the last four years, it averaged 105s. 5d. On the basis of this data, the Committee made a diagnosis of the situation which is best summed up in the words of the report.

"Your Committee are of the opinion, that so great a degree of dependence on foreign countries for a sufficient supply of food, and so great an advance in the price of wheat as is hereby proved, require the interposition of Parliament without further delay, in order that some remedy may be applied to evils of such great prejudice to the public welfare."[2]

With this object before it, the Committee set out to discover the Parliamentary measures which would secure an adequate supply of grain from British land and, at the same time, reduce the price of grain to consumers.

[1] The report of the Committee on the Corn Laws of Great Britain will be found in Hansard, *Parliamentary Debates*, 1st Series, Vol. 25, Appendix, p. 55.
[2] *Ibid.*, p. 55.

Enquiries were made of the Board of Agriculture and the Farming Society of Ireland to ascertain what were the possibilities of growing more grain in the United Kingdom. The reply from the Board of Agriculture showed, the Committee said, "that there had been a great increase of tillage during the last ten years; that the land now in tillage is capable of being made much more productive by extension of the improved system of cultivation, and that much land now in grass is fit to be converted into tillage."[1]

The information obtained from the Farming Society of Ireland and the testimony of the witnesses led the Committee to conclude that the situation was much the same in Ireland. It suggested, therefore, that Irish farmers be encouraged to continue increasing their production of grain, especially wheat, since this would make it unnecessary for the English to plough up much of their fine pasture land. Ireland could concentrate on growing grain and England could specialise in dairy produce and live stock breeding. This would be entirely satisfactory to both parties, it thought, since the Irish would take payment for their grain in manufactured goods and the English consumer would have both grain and meat at moderate prices. The feasibility of this plan was demonstrated by the statistics on exports of grain from Ireland to England. Since the establishment of free trade between the two countries in 1806, the value of Irish grain imports had increased from one-seventh to one-third of the

[1] Hansard. S. 1, Vol. 25, Appendix, p. 56.

total coming into England from all countries. Should this rapid growth in production continue, it concluded, Great Britain would no longer need to depend on foreign countries for any of her supply of grain.[1]

The Committee, to discover what legislation was needed to bring this about, next turned its attention to the Corn Laws. An examination of grain prices in England following the adoption of the protective principles established by the Acts of 1670 and 1689 clearly showed what was the proper course for Parliament to take respecting the Corn Trade. It might be supposed that such high protection would result in high prices for grain but the evidence proved, on the contrary, that these two acts were followed by moderate and stable prices. The Acts of 1773 and 1791 had altered this system by giving less protection to agriculture. The result was that the prices of grain had risen; England had become an importing rather than an exporting country; and the poor had been made to suffer severely from the great fluctuations in the prices of necessaries. Furthermore, the experience of England since the Wars began showed the unwisdom of depending on foreign supplies of grain.

To remedy all of these difficulties, it would be necessary for Parliament to enact a new set of Corn Laws. The Committee presented, therefore, several Resolutions for the consideration of the House which would, if enacted, enable Great Britain to dispense with foreign grain, and, at the same time, keep prices

[1] Hansard, S. 1, Vol. 25, Appendix, pp. 57–8.

both steady and moderate. A brief summary of these suggestions will show how this seemingly impossible accomplishment was to be achieved.[1]

1. In the future, the importation and exportation of each kind of grain should be regulated by an average price for the whole kingdom made up from the prices in the twelve maritime districts of England and Wales, the four maritime districts of Scotland and the four maritime districts of Ireland.

2. The extension of a bounty on exports should be abandoned for this reason: "If the regulating price for allowing importation is made a very high one, it is the best possible protection the grower can have."[2] Exports should not be prohibited, however, until the price of wheat rose above 90s. 2d. the quarter.

3. The prices and duties regulating imports should be fixed as follows.[3] When wheat was under 105s. 2d. the high duty of 24s. 3d. should be paid; between 105s. 2d. and under 135s. 2d. a medium duty of 2s. 6d.; at, or above, 135s. 2d. a nominal charge of 6d. was to be paid. These prices were to stand until February 1, 1814. They were to be replaced before this time by other prices calculated by the Receiver of Corn Returns from the price data for January 1, 1814. This same revision was to be carried out in each succeeding year according to the following procedure.

The export prices for the different kinds of grain

---

[1] The Resolutions are found in the Report, Hansard, S. 1, Vol. 25, Appendix, p. 63.
[2] *Ibid.*, p. 62.   [3] *Ibid.*, p. 63.

were to be calculated each year by adding one-seventh to the average price for the last twenty years. Prices for imports were to be fixed in the same manner except that one-third instead of one-seventh should be added to the average to determine the point at which the high duty should go into effect. Five-sevenths was to be added for fixing the upper limit of the middle duty.

4. All Corn Laws then in effect should be repealed.

5. All importations of foreign flour or meal into Great Britain should be prohibited.

It was quite evident that the Committee intended to maintain the prices of grain at their war-time level if legislation would do it. The proposals also showed considerable bias in favour of the Irish farmers. They were to be given a monopoly of the English market, except for periods of famine prices, with the option of selling their grain elsewhere should they see fit to do so. Both the Irish and English farmers, it thought, would benefit by the proposed system of calculating the average prices for imports and exports because adding a certain percentage each year to the average price for the past twenty years would tend to counteract any further inflation of the currency. Lest it should be suspected of sponsoring class legislation, the Committee attempted to win the support of the English consumers by holding out the lure of "moderate and steady" prices.

This rather thinly veiled argument did not convince many English bread-eaters of the good intentions of the Committee. Parnell,[1] sensing the unpopularity of the high import prices proposed, decided to modify the Resolutions with a suggestion of his own. When the Report came up for discussion in the Commons in June 1813, he suggested that the price under which imports would pay the high duty should be calculated by adding one-fifth to the average price of the last twenty years instead of one-third. This would make the regulating price for wheat 95s. per quarter instead of 105s., but in place of the high duty at this price he would charge only the nominal sum of 1s. For every drop of 1s. below 95s., however, the duty was to increase by an equal amount until at 85s. it would amount to 11s. which he thought would afford sufficient protection.

Lest even the new price and duties on imports still seem too high to the English consumers, he went to some trouble to show how they would benefit from the proposed legislation. In the first place, he pointed out, there would be security against scarcity such as necessitated the payment of such large sums of money for foreign corn in the past. This money, if spent at home, would have enabled the country to raise its own food and there would no longer have been any necessity for England to depend on her most powerful enemy, France. Had there ever been an instance in history, he asked, of a large nation continuing with undiminished vigour to support four or five millions of its people on

[1] The speech of Sir Henry Parnell can be found in Hansard, S. 1, Vol. 26, pp. 644–59.

imported corn, to say nothing of the fact that this corn came in foreign ships and that the carrying was adding to the naval strength of the enemy?[1]

In the second place, the prices of grain would fluctuate to a much less extent if the proposals were enacted. They were based on the principle established by the legislation of 1670 and 1689 which had proved eminently successful in this respect. This greater stability of prices would be a boon to the labourer and his family, for wages always had a tendency to lag in a period of rising prices. Certainly, he said, the labourer should support the recommendations.

Thirdly, and this is the most curious of his arguments, the effect of the measures would not be to raise the prices of grain. This might, it was true, be their effect in the short run. But, in the long run, the high duties by stimulating production and competition among the farmers would actually bring about lower prices.

Neither the Report of the Committee nor the ingenious arguments of Parnell seems to have made a great impression on the House. Various objections were raised against considering a revision of the Corn Laws in that session. Not a few considered the remaining time as inadequate for a full discussion. Some were inclined to think the information at hand both scanty and deficient. It was also suggested that the people, who had been

[1] The speech of Sir Henry Parnell, Hansard, S. 1, Vol. 26, p. 646.

faced with famine prices for the last four years, would strongly object when they were told that it was proposed to continue these prices with the aid of Parliament.

During a subsequent discussion [1] of the Corn Laws on June 21, the Commons agreed to the Resolution which proposed the calculation of the regulating prices for exports and imports from the average of prices in the maritime districts of Ireland, Scotland and England. The lateness of the session precluded further debate and Parnell finally moved that consideration of the other Resolutions be postponed until the following year.[2]

The scanty support which the Resolutions had received in the House did not present a bright outlook for the schemes of the Committee. But in the discussion throughout the country which followed the debates, it was apparent that the idea of high protective duties giving the home producers a monopoly had " caught on " among the farmers. The slogan of " steady prices " was adopted by the high protectionists and it was evident that the argument holding all which was paid to the foreigner as lost would be worked for all it was worth.[3]

2. THE BATTLE OF THE CORN LAWS

While Parnell's arguments were being disseminated by the high protectionists, a series of events occurred which won them the ardent support

[1] Hansard, S. 1, Vol. 26, p. 812.   [2] *Ibid.*, p. 986.
[3] See Smart, Wm., *Economic Annals of the Nineteenth Century*, p. 407.

of practically all the landlords in the Kingdom. The harvest of 1813 proved to be one of the most abundant in the history of the country. As a result, the price of wheat, which had risen to the unheard of amount of 155s. per quarter in August 1812, fell to 75s. 10d. for the week of December 25, 1813—a little less than half of its former price.[1] The prices of other kinds of grain suffered a like drop. The corresponding decline in incomes of farmers and those landlords, who had not rented lands under long leases, gave them a lively interest in the Resolutions before Parliament. By the time the debate was resumed in May 1814, it was evident that Parnell would have strong support.

This same series of events brought relief to another class of people, the workers. For four years in a row they had been faced with famine prices for bread and, from their point of view, an abundant harvest necessitated anything but remedial legislation. It might be expected then that, while the landlords in Parliament would favour the Resolutions the more strongly, the workers and manufacturing classes would be just as decidedly against them. But the relative strength of the two could not be tested politically for the legislature was controlled by the landed classes.

It must not be supposed that there was no one at all in Parliament to represent the labouring and manufacturing classes. Indeed, the debates in this year have been characterised as " The Battle of the

[1] Weekly averages of prices of wheat from 1800 to 1814 can be found in Galpin, *op. cit.*, Appendix No. 5, pp. 213–19.

Corn Laws."[1] This battle was waged mainly between the opposing interests of the agriculturalists and the manufacturing classes, for the latter had a few staunch defenders in both Houses. As a matter of fact, there were at least three different shades of opinion expressed by members of the Commons. At one extreme, there were the high protectionists. Between them and the free-traders stood a group who favoured moderate protection, or at the most, a temporary relief measure. The ranks of the advocates of laissez-faire were composed of a few members from manufacturing districts and the " political economists." The latter were not the only ones who appealed to the science of political economy in the ensuing debates. Both sides drew on *The Wealth of Nations* for supporting arguments. Since the debates of 1814 throw considerable light both on English agricultural conditions and the efficacy of tariff revision as a method of farm relief, it will be worth while to review briefly the major arguments presented pro and con.

It was Mr. Rose,[2] a representative of the moderate group of protectionists, who obtained the first hearing after Parnell had moved the adoption of the Resolution permitting the free export of grain. He did not confine himself to the one matter of the regulation of exports but made a general attack on the Report of the Committee of 1813. First of all he voiced his objection to the import prices and

[1] See Smart, Wm., *op. cit.*, p. 407.
[2] For the speech of Mr. Rose see Hansard, S. 1, Vol. 27, pp. 665 ff.

duties proposed. They would, in his estimation, give the home producer too much of a monopoly. The growers, he said, were entitled to reasonable protection, but the interests of the consumer must also be considered. The problem, as he put it, was

"to come to a determination of what the prices should be at which importation should be allowed and exportation restrained; taking it for granted that no one now entertains the remotest idea of an entirely free trade in corn which would be equally mischievous to both grower and consumer."[1]

There could be no doubt, in his estimation, that, should the farmer be left entirely without protection, foreign producers would flood the market with their grain. He had information to the effect that wheat was selling in Dantzig at 36s. 3d. the quarter and that the charges on imports were as follows: [2]

In War:	s.	In Peace:	s.
Shipping charges	10	Insurance	2
French Licence	10	Freight	14
Insurance	17	Shipping Charges	10
Freight	45		
Total	82	Total	26

Under these circumstances, he calculated that 80s. would offer sufficient protection to the grower in times of peace. Anything above that would greatly injure the consumers and manufacturers. Since wages fluctuated with the price of necessaries, domestic industries would be at a disadvantage in

[1] Hansard, S. 1, Vol. 27, pp. 694–5.
[2] The table can be found in *Ibid.*, p. 695.

competition with foreigners who employed labour where bread was cheaper.

As for the argument that higher duties would stimulate production and eventually lower prices, he could not see how any increase in protection now would greatly increase production when the famine prices of the last four years did not bring into use all of the available land. " The Committee," he said, " hold out to captivate one description of people on the expectation that by increased production bread will become cheap ; and, to another, that by raising the prices of importation and lessening those for exportation, corn will become dearer."[1] It could hardly expect, he pointed out, to fool anyone by such talk. The real object of the Resolutions was to raise the prices of grain.

Parnell[2] replied to Mr. Rose in a long speech in which he reiterated many of his former arguments. He wished the House to know that neither he nor the Committee intended to secure excessive protection for agriculture. Accordingly, he proposed a new Resolution fixing the price for wheat imports at 84s.[3] But, if that was found too high, he was ready to concur in whatever the House might consider proper. Whatever price might be fixed, there was no truth in the contention that it would determine the home price of wheat. And, since the measure would not have the effect of raising the price of wheat, it would not cause the manufacturers any inconvenience. Furthermore, he would not

---

[1] From the speech of Mr. Rose, Hansard, S. 1, Vol. 27, p. 705.
[2] *Ibid.*, pp. 708 ff.   [3] *Ibid.*, p. 709.

accept the theory that wages were fixed in accordance with the price of bread; they were determined by the demand for and the supply of labour.

The manufacturers, he argued, were short-sighted in their opposition to the Resolutions. They favoured free trade in grain but they did not stop to consider the fact that, of those who furnished supplies outside of England, the Irish took by far the largest share of their pay in manufactured goods. "Surely, then," he said, "it was not asking too much of this country to purchase corn from Ireland in preference to Poland." [1]

But, apart from selfish interests, the English manufacturer should consider Ireland as an agricultural exporting country. It was unfair to deprive them of free access to foreign markets just as it would be to prohibit the exportation of manufactured goods. One of the Irish grain merchants had informed him that the existing laws had prevented his filling large orders of wheat for the Brazils only last autumn. "It was very curious to remark that, while corn was a mere drug in Ireland, in Jamaica they were so much in want of it that the inhabitants had addressed the Prince Regent on the subject." [2]

The "political economists," he said, had taken the side of the manufacturers on theoretical grounds alone. They had made their slogan, "Buy in the cheapest markets," but they had not stopped to consider the actual effect the introduction of free

---

[1] Hansard, S. 1, Vol. 27, p. 716. [2] *Ibid.*, p. 716.

FARM RELIEF IN ENGLAND, 1813-1852   53

trade would have on the wealth of the country. To permit foreign grain to enter free of duty would mean the ruin of a great many farmers and landlords. It was true that the imports of grain might be paid for by exports of manufactured goods. But the question was: "whether any sound system of policy can justify the general derangement of all that vast stock of labour, skill and capital, which is vested in agriculture, for the uncertain result of adding, in some measure, to the general wealth of the country."[1] He was convinced that, if Adam Smith could now give his opinion on the subject, the great economist would include protection for agriculture under those exceptions to free trade which he made in his works.[2]

After some further debate, the House approved the Resolution which called for the repeal of the laws prohibiting the exportation of grain, meal, malt and flour.[3] This, it will be recalled, was one of the things sought by the Irish landlords. Parnell's speeches had evidently made some impression. The next object on his programme was to secure a comparatively high duty on foreign imports.

The Resolution on the import trade as amended read: the duty of 24s. 3d. should be paid when wheat was under 84s. per quarter; at, or above, 84s. but under 87s. the duty should be 2s. 6d.; when at

---
[1] Hansard, S. 1, Vol. 27, p. 714.
[2] Parnell enumerates the exceptional cases in which Adam Smith agreed that import duties would be justified in *Ibid.*, pp. 713–15.
[3] *Ibid.*, p. 722.

or above 87s., imports were to be admitted on payment of the nominal sum of 2s. 6d. the quarter. This did not suit the ideas of Mr. Huskisson who rose to propose an amendment.[1]

The two great objects of the House were, he said: (1) To render the country independent of foreign supplies of grain; (2) To keep the prices of grain as nearly steady as possible. The first of these would have been accomplished if the sixty millions sterling, which had been paid for grain imports during the war, had been spent at home on improving the production of grain. It would not require any very great increase in production to make the country self-sufficient, for Great Britain had never drawn more than one-tenth, or one-twelfth, of her grain supply from foreign sources.

The second purpose of the House could, he thought, be accomplished by raising the import prices. They most certainly should not be lowered as some members had proposed. If protection were withdrawn from agriculture after the artificial restraints on trade during the Wars had, by raising prices, made the country nearly independent, farming would go back to its former state. Indeed, the fall in the prices of grain since the harvest of 1813 had forced the farmers to lay off their labourers in many cases. He favoured the principle of the Resolution before the House but he thought the prices proposed would give too much of a monopoly to the home grower. The amendment he proposed

---

[1] Mr. Huskisson's speech can be found in Hansard, S. 1, Vol. 27, p. 722.

would leave importation open at all times, and retain the price of 63s. as that at which the prohibitory duty of 24s. 3d. should operate. When the price of corn rose 1s. so the duty should fall; for example, when corn was at 64s. the duty should be 23s. 3d. and so on; so that at 86s. there would be no duty at all.[1]

Parnell accepted this amendment and the debate continued. As the session wore on, the discussions became more animated on all sides. The large carry-over from the previous year's crop, together with the bright prospects for another good harvest in the fall, caused prices to drop still further. Foreign grain was coming into the country in considerable quantity and would not be checked until the price had fallen to 63s. One writer has succinctly described the situation of the landed classes as follows:

" The landlords were caught, as it were, on a vast speculation on high and higher prices. To take advantage of the war prices, they had enclosed greedily and begun to cultivate land that would pay at those high prices but not at any ordinary ones. They had, moreover, launched out into extravagant living, and burdened their estates with settlements. The farmers were in the same boat. Presuming on the continuance of the high prices, they had sunk their capital in new lands and improvements and renewed their leases at high rents which they would not be able to pay if prices came down. They also had raised their standard of living." [2]

---

[1] Hansard, S. 1, Vol. 27, p. 725. This was the famous sliding scale principle which was incorporated in the Corn Law of 1828.
[2] Smart, *op. cit.*, p 408.

From every correspondent of *The Farmer's Magazine* came an appeal that the legislature take some step to avert the impending ruin.

But the opponents of the Resolution seemed determined to prevent the passage of any measure during that session of Parliament. Some declared the information before the House to be inadequate; more time should be taken to assemble data and discuss the Resolutions before passing any permanent measure. The Ministry, they said, was pledged to see that the Bank of England resumed specie payments after the Wars. Considering the possibilities of a great change in the currency, no permanent measure should be enacted at present. Another group argued that, since the taxation policy of the Ministry had not been put on a peace basis, it would be impossible for duties and prices to be set which would come very close to equalising costs of production between the foreign and home producers.

Parnell did his best to avoid delay. Huskisson predicted a panic among the farmers within the next year if some measure was not passed. " There should be no hesitation in giving protection to agriculture," he said, " when the whole of our commercial and economical system was one of artificial expedients."[1]

The hopes of the protectionists for the early passage of a Corn Bill were practically shattered by the storm of protest which broke out in the

---

[1] Mr. Huskisson's speech as given in Hansard, S. 1, Vol. 27, p. 920.

country. On May 27 the manufacturing towns showered the House with petitions against a change in the Corn Laws. The Journals of the House of Commons record over 170 petitions presented against, with practically none for, a change.[1] The tenants do not seem to have been greatly interested, if one can judge by the absence of statements from them in support of the proposed revision of the import duties. It may have been that they felt confident that the landlords in Parliament would look out for their interests without encouragement.

The Ministry,[2] which had been supporting the proposed revisions, finally decided not to press the measures. The Chancellor of the Exchequer moved to refer the petitions to a Select Committee " with the intention and hope, that, if the Committee could make their report in due time, some legislative measure might be founded upon it in the course of the present session."[3] It was also directed to examine the Corn Laws then in force and, if they were found wanting in any respect, it should bring the House suggestions for properly securing the interests of agriculture.[4]

The Chancellor of the Exchequer was destined to be disappointed if he expected the Committee to do so much work in the little time left in the session and still give the House the opportunity to pass a

---

[1] Smart, Wm., *op. cit.*, p. 414.
[2] The Prime Minister was then Lord Liverpool, a Tory, who held office from 1812 to 1827.
[3] Mr. Vansittart was Chancellor of the Exchequer. The quotation is taken from his speech as recorded in Hansard, S. 1, Vol. 27, p. 1084.
[4] *Ibid.*, p. 1085.

bill. It finally reported in the last of July without saying a word about the petitions, but considerable attention had been given to the other instructions.[1] It found that the increasing population and "growing opulence of the Kingdom," aided by the impediments to importation during the Wars, had been the means of encouraging a great deal of enclosing and reclamation of waste lands. Should there be no restrictions placed on the competition of the foreign growers, these improvements would receive a serious check and prevent a great deal of waste land from being brought under tillage. Granting that protection was necessary, the question to be answered was that of setting the price at which imports would be permitted. It found that during the last twenty years money rents and the expenses of cultivation had doubled. Under these circumstances, it calculated that 80s. per quarter would be the lowest price which would afford adequate remuneration to the wheat growers. Indeed, if the "cold clay, or, waste and inferior lands" were to continue under cultivation, and a considerable proportion of wheat was now grown on such lands, the price would have to be still higher. This land, if forced out of tillage, would be a loss to both farmers and consumers for it could not be turned to any other use for some little time.

Shortly after the Committee reported, the session came to an end. While this long struggle was going on in the Commons over the import prices, the

[1] The Report does not seem to have been printed in Hansard. It can be found in *The Farmer's Magazine* for 1814 p. 445.

Lords gave their approval to the measure which had been passed in the lower House permitting the free exportation of grain without a bounty. This was the extent of the legislative accomplishments for the year.

3. THE RESUMPTION OF THE BATTLE, 1815

The harvest of 1814, while not so abundant as that of 1813, proved to be a good one and prices of grain continued to move downward. But they did not fall far enough to bring the existing Corn Laws into effective operation against foreign imports until January 1815. Consequently, nearly 700,000 quarters of wheat and meal came into the country in 1814.[1] This was a great source of worry to the farmers and landlords and they persuaded the Ministry to set aside all other business in order to secure the early passage of a new Corn Law in the session of 1815. In fact, it was a representative of the Government who brought forth a new set of Resolutions based on the report of the Committee.[2] He denied that it was the intention of the Ministry to favour one class at the expense of another. Protection was fully justified because it would free the country from any worry over the uncertainty of foreign supplies of grain. This would benefit everyone. He, therefore, moved a set of Resolutions which, if enacted, would attain this object. They were: (1) the present system of warehousing should

---

[1] See Porter, G. R., *Progress of the Nation*, Vol. I, p. 156.
[2] These Resolutions were moved by the Hon. Frederick Robinson, Vice-President of the Board of Trade. His speech can be found in Hansard, S. 1, Vol. 29, p. 798.

60 AGRICULTURAL DEPRESSION AND

be continued; and (2) the prices regulating the imports of corn should be:

	For Foreign Imports. Per quarter. s.	For North American Colonies. Per quarter. s.
Wheat	80	67
Rye, Pease and Beans	53	44
Barley, Beer or Bigg	40	33
Oats	26	22

When the home prices were higher than these, imports should be admitted free.

(3) Once the prices had been determined by the Inspector General, imports should be allowed to come in from France, Flanders and Germany during the following six weeks, providing the home price did not fall below 80s. If this should happen, imports from these ports should be stopped immediately. Other foreign supplies of grain should be admitted for three months, once the price rose above 80s., no matter how the home price was affected.

The arguments of the Ministry were answered by Mr. Philips, a free-trader.[1] He wished to remind the House of the exact object of its deliberations, lest they should forget the interests of all classes. The issue, he said, had been squarely put by the Hon. Mr. Robinson. There could be no doubt that the Ministry intended to provide a remedy for the low price of grain. "That which all ages and countries had considered as a great national benefit was now discovered to be a great evil against which we were imperiously called to

[1] Mr. Philips' speech can be found in Hansard, S. 1, Vol. 29, pp. 808 ff.

legislate in self-defence."[1] Should the price of grain be raised by such legislation, it would undoubtedly put English manufacturers at a disadvantage in foreign markets, for it would necessitate higher wages.

The idea of making the country self-sufficient could only be realised at a great expense. It was unnecessary to do this anyway for other countries would benefit quite as much by a system of free trade as would England, and it would, therefore, be to the interests of all to avoid political difficulties. There were economic forces also to be considered which could not be thwarted by legislation. Had not Napoleon failed to cut off the supply of grain when it was most needed during the Wars?

Should Parliament pass a measure now, it will soon be called on again to pass another. For what might be a remunerative price at one time would not be adequate in a few years. The great fall in prices, he maintained, had thrown the landlords and farmers into a panic-stricken frame of mind. Some temporary relief might be advisable but there was no justification for adopting a permanent measure to cure a transitory injury.

In accordance with Mr. Philips' idea, Mr. Baring proposed a new set of Resolutions calculated to give the farmers only temporary protection at high prices.[2] He suggested fixing the price for wheat imports at 75s. the quarter for the period of one year. In each succeeding year the price

[1] Hansard, S. 1, Vol. 29, p. 809.
[2] *Ibid.*, p. 829.

would be lowered by 2s. until the old regulating price of 63s. should be reached. This, he calculated, would give the farmers and landlords a chance to acclimatise themselves to peace conditions.

During the course of the debates, a large number of petitions were presented to the House voicing strong protests against the proposals of the Ministry. In fact, it was the largest number in history of Parliament in the estimation of Lord Grey.[1] The large cities and manufacturing towns were practically all represented. The petition from Bristol was signed by 40,000 and the House of Lords received one from Manchester signed by 52,000 The people of Liverpool and London each sent in their protest backed by 48,000, and 40,000 signatures respectively. "The people," said Sir Robert Peel, "were not to be cajoled by such arguments as that the Bill would give them cheap bread; they knew the thing was impossible. If the measure passed the manufactures of the towns would be destroyed." [2]

The absence of petitions from the tenants is again noticeable. According to some of the landlords in Parliament, their farmers had not shown any interest in the matter.[3] Those who held land under long leases must certainly have been interested; the others could, of course, give up their land should prices continue to fall, or re-rent it on more favourable terms. In any case, the landlords

---

[1] Smart, Wm., *Economic Annals of the Nineteenth Century*, pp. 450–1.
[2] *Ibid.*, p. 451.   [3] *Ibid.*, p. 451.

would probably stand to lose for, if prices fell, rents would probably go unpaid. This fact accounts for their greater interest in the matter.

In spite of the unmistakable unpopularity of the Bill framed on the Resolutions which Robinson had presented, the strong government majority bore down all amendments. The final vote was taken on March 3 and the Bill passed by 218 to 56.[1] In the House of Lords it met the opposition of a small group of peers. They, of course, were greatly outnumbered by the advocates of high protection but voiced their protest in a signed statement which was entered in the Journals of the House of Lords.[2]

There was no doubt after the clash over the Corn Laws that a good many Englishmen had begun to doubt the arguments purporting to prove the general benefits to be derived from protection for agriculture. Some of the more critical thought that the Bill of 1815 would have no beneficial effects even in the case of the farmers. Protection from foreign competition, they argued, would not be sufficient to maintain domestic prices and, therefore, the farmers would be fooled entirely. At any rate, they pointed out, it was naive to expect that such a bill would make the country self-sufficient and, at the same time, steady prices, when the country no longer grew sufficient grain to meet its own needs. The discussion of these questions, and other matters affecting the condition of the farmers, will be taken up in the following chapter.

[1] Hansard, S. 1, Vol. 30, p. 125. [2] *Ibid.*, p. 263.

CHAPTER III

AGRICULTURAL DISTRESS, 1815-16

ENGLAND emerged victorious from the Napoleonic Wars in 1815. But she paid the price of victory with a huge National Debt, excessive taxation, loss of foreign trade, a system of unstable currency and credit, and an army of unemployed workers who voiced their discontent in rioting. Peace necessitated readjustments which proved costly to all classes but probably none were harder hit than the agriculturists.

Prices fell; land values dropped precipitously; farming stock became a drug on the market; and in their adversity the landlords and tenants found themselves loaded down with heavy taxes and increasing poor-rates. Once again they appealed to Parliament.

In this chapter an attempt will be made to analyse the factors which precipitated the fall in agricultural prices and to give a picture of the farmer's situation in the dark years of 1815 and 1816. The reliance of the landed classes on legislative relief will again be noted in their appeals to Parliament. A brief summary of the politicians' diagnoses of the causes of the distress, and the

FARM RELIEF IN ENGLAND, 1813–1852   65

proper measures to be taken, will show the differences of opinion as to what, if anything, should be done. In conclusion, there will be a brief summary of the legislative measures passed for the relief of the landed classes.

1. THE FALL IN AGRICULTURAL AND NON-AGRICULTURAL PRICES, 1814–16

The indices of Professor Silberling show that the general price level reached a peak in 1814 and then fell approximately 32 per cent. between this year and 1817.[1] It will be recalled from the data in Chapter II that the prices of grain reached a high point in 1812. After the harvest of 1813, they fell precipitously until in 1815 they were, in most cases, about half of what they had been in 1812. The prices of wool, beef, mutton, and cheese according to the following table [2] also show a decline after 1814.

There was, at the time, a good deal of disagreement as to just what was the prime cause of this drop in the general price level after 1814. Later writers have also failed to come to any general agreement, but this does not seem strange considering the number of economic forces which were involved.

[1] See Chart 1, Chapter II, for Professor Silberling's indices. The calculation is based on his index numbers given in the *Review of Economic Statistics Supplement*, Preliminary Vol. 5, p. 232.

[2] This table is taken from data compiled by G. N. Driver for private circulation among land surveyors and was published in the *Journal of the Statistical Society*, Vol. I, pp. 56–7. No source references are given but the prices have been checked as far as possible with other available tables and no very great discrepancies were found.

Table I

Annual Average Prices of Agricultural Commodities, 1810–22

Year.	Wheat per qtr.		Rye per qtr.		Barley per qtr.		Oats per qtr.		Wool per lb. South-down.		Wool per lb. Lincoln-shire.		Beef and Mutton per lb.	Cheese per lb.
	s.	d.	s.	d.	s.	d.	s.	d.	s.	d.	s.	d.	d.	d.
1810 . . .	103	3	56	8	47	9	29	4	2	1	1	1½	8½	8
1811 . . .	92	5	46	1	41	9	28	10	2	1	0	11	8¾	8¼
1812 . . .	122	8	76	3	66	6	44	0	2	2	1	2	8¼	8½
1813 . . .	106	6	69	9	58	3	39	3	2	4	1	3	8¾	8¾
1814 . . .	72	1	43	4	37	4	26	6	2	6	1	7½	9½	8¾
1815 . . .	63	8	37	0	29	9	23	9	1	10	1	11½	8¼	8
1816 . . .	76	2	41	0	30	9	21	9	1	10	1	1½	7¼	6½
1817 . . .	94	0	58	9	48	6	31	2	2	0	1	3½	6	5½
1818 . . .	83	8	62	8	51	6	31	2	2	0½	2	0	7¼	6
1819 . . .	72	3	52	7	45	6	27	8	1	6	1	5	7¾	8
1820 . . .	65	10	41	10	33	4	23	10	1	6	1	6	7½	7
1821 . . .	54	5	33	0	25	11	19	3	1	4	1	1½	6¾	5½
1822 . . .	43	3	20	3	21	3	17	7	1	6	1	0½	5	4½

Some current opinion was expressed to the effect that preparations for the resumption of cash payments by the Bank of England, and the necessary readjustments to peace conditions, accounted for the agricultural and business depression in 1815–16. To show that the currency had very little to do with the situation and that whatever alterations were made in it were the result, and not the cause, of the fall in prices, Thomas Tooke wrote his famous History of Prices.[1] He argues that supply factors were sufficient to account for both the agricultural and commercial distress. In the case of the farmer, the abundant harvests of 1813 and 1815 coupled with the large importation of 1814 produced an overstocked market from which there was no relief until in the second quarter of 1816. It was true, he admitted, that the fall in agricultural prices caused the country banks great losses, but the reduction in their currency was decidedly a result, not a cause. As for the industrial and commercial depression, he was convinced that it was the result of: (1) peace conditions which brought greater freedom of trade and, therefore, lower costs of transportation; (2) lower costs of production in the case of manufactured goods; and (3) the reaction from over-speculation in goods for shipment to the Continent which had caused them to be sold cheaper abroad than at home. That the currency, as far as the Bank of England was concerned, could have had

[1] See his *History of Prices*, Vol. II, Chapter VI, for his price analysis for the period 1814–18.

little or nothing to do with the fall in prices was evidenced, he thought, by the fact that the amount of its note circulation was actually greater in 1814, 1815, and 1816 than it had been in 1813.[1]

Another analysis which agreed in part with Tooke's was given by McCulloch.[2] In his estimation the fall in grain prices was precipitated by the unusually good harvest of 1813. The situation was made still worse by the large importations in 1814 due to the delay in passing the Corn Law. This fall in prices caused great losses to the farmers and the country banks, from whom they had borrowed heavily, began to press for the repayment of loans. Out of necessity the farmers had thrown large quantities of grain and stock on the market for what they would bring, and many farmers, in spite of their sacrifices, were unable to meet their obligations. The country banks, as a consequence, found it necessary to curtail credit and many of them were forced into insolvency. The failure of these banks resulted in an estimated reduction of £20,000,000 in the amount of country bank-notes. The depression in agriculture and industry in general was, then, due in part to deflation. That this process had been carried out to a considerable extent was proven, he argued, by the increased value of the pound in the foreign exchange market.

---

[1] Tooke, Thomas, *History of Prices*, Vol. II. See Chapter VI, pp. 55-9, for a summary of his conclusions.

[2] See an article in *The Farmer's Magazine*, Vol. 18, p. 31, Feb. 1817, based on an Essay by J. R. McCulloch, "The Question of Reducing the Interest on the National Debt."

It seems to be clear that the original fall in agricultural prices was due in large part to the abundant crop of 1813. But the further decline in grain prices and other farm produce was complicated by the simultaneous operation of a number of economic forces. To sum up the situation, the factors bearing on the supply of and the demand for agricultural produce are here listed. On the supply side, the large harvests in 1813 and in 1815; the forced sales of produce and stock; the importations of 1814; and the possibilities of being able to get future supplies of foreign grain cheaply, must be considered. The demand was affected by the failure of 92 country banks and the suspension of cash payments by 240 of these;[1] the depression in manufacturing and commerce which caused a great deal of unemployment; the decline in purchases by the government of food, clothing and equipment for armies; and the large number of returned soldiers and sailors without jobs or purchasing power.

2. THE DISTRESS OF TENANTS AND LANDLORDS

Whatever may have been the cause, there is little doubt that the fall in agricultural prices occasioned a great deal of distress among the landed classes in 1815 and 1816. The small farmers, who had borrowed from the country banks to add to their holdings of land, found the financial strain too great and were forced to sell out for whatever they could get. This tended to accentuate the

[1] McCulloch, J. R., *Commercial Dictionary*, p. 78.

concentration of ownership of land, for only the most wealthy of landlords were in a position to take advantage of the opportunities. Tenants, holding land under long leases at rents based on war-time prices, had to sell their stock to pay rents and, finally, were forced to give up their farms. Those who had leased land for a shorter period of time quit and put the burden on their landlords. The latter found tenants unable to fulfil their contracts and were forced to take over the management of their own lands. Land values dropped precipitously; rents went unpaid, or were scaled down in many cases; but the fixed expenses of the landlords continued.

The loud cries of distress from the landed classes attracted the attention of the Board of Agriculture. With the intention of securing authentic information on the amount and extent of the distress it sent out a questionnaire to its correspondents in the United Kingdom.[1] Since these replies afford one of the best and most complete sources of information on the condition of agriculture in these years, a brief summary of them will be given.

The questions which the Board asked were: [2]

1. "Are any farms in your neighbourhood unoccupied by tenants; and have landlords, in consequence, been obliged to take them into their own hands?"
2. "Have any tenants, within your knowledge, given notice to their landlords, of quitting their farms at Ladyday, or any other period?"

[1] An account of the findings of the Board is given in *The Farmer's Magazine*, Vol. 17, Nov. 1816, pp. 465-80.
[2] *Ibid.*, p. 466.

FARM RELIEF IN ENGLAND, 1813-1852

3. "Have any farms been lately re-let at an abatement of rent; and if so, what is the proportion of such abatement?"
4. "What circumstances, denoting the distress of the farmers, have come to your knowledge, which may not be included under the above queries?"
5. "Is the present distress greater on arable, or on grass farms?"
6. "Have flock-farms suffered equally with others?"
7. "Does the county in which you reside, suffer from a diminished circulation of paper?"
8. "What is the state of the labouring poor; and what is the proportion of poor-rates compared with the years 1811 and 1812?"
9. "What remedies occur to you for alleviating these difficulties?"

Three hundred and twenty-six letters in all were received in reply to these questions and the writer for *The Farmer's Magazine* has the following comment to make regarding their importance.[1]

"The exertions of no private individual, or local society, could have accumulated so great a body of interesting facts and opinions; facts so well authenticated, and opinions so well entitled to attention—supported as they are by the names of men among the most eminent, both for their general knowledge of the state of the country, and for their experience in the practice of agriculture."

He goes on to point out that the opinions expressed represented not a particular class or section of the country but practically all of the agricultural counties of Great Britain.

---

[1] *The Farmer's Magazine*, Vol. 17, p. 467.

In answer to the first question, the Board received three hundred and thirteen replies. They may be briefly summarised as follows:

Letters mentioning farms unoccupied by tenants, being thrown on the landlords hands . . 168
Letters in which no such want of occupancy occurs [1] 127
Letters in which farms are stated to have been uncultivated for want of being occupied by landlords 18

In reply to the second question dealing with notices to quit, the letters received may be summarised thus: [2]

Letters in which the expression is, "many" farmers have given notice to quit . . . 103
Letters in which the expressions are "several," or "a few" have given notice to quit . . 111
Letters in which the expression is, "all that can have given notice to quit" 37
Letters in which the expression is, "none have given notice to quit" 71

---

[1] It was observed that the 127 letters showing no want of occupancy should not be taken as an indication of prosperity since they showed, at the same time, evidence most descriptive of the agricultural distress. Indeed, 64 of them state that notices to quit had been given. They also declare a large quantity of land to be uncultivated. *The Farmer's Magazine*, Vol. 17, p. 467.

[2] The writer for *The Farmer's Magazine* makes the following comment on these letters. "It is scarcely necessary to remark, that until the present period of declension commenced, such an idea, as giving notice to quit a farm except for the purpose of hiring a better one, may be said to have been almost unknown in the kingdom; and no circumstance can more clearly mark the present degradation of the employment, than these notices to quit." *Ibid.*, p. 467.

There were 212 returns specifying the relative reduction in rents. The average of these was 25 per cent. and, estimating the land rents of the Kingdom at £36 millions, the reduction would amount to £9 millions as one year's loss. To this should be added the amount of unpaid rents which was stated in many letters to be large.[1]

The letters on the General State of Husbandry went into considerable detail. Many of them mention cases of bankruptcies, seizures, executions and imprisonments for debts. They also state that many farmers had become parish paupers and, in general, indicate a discontinuance of improvements of every kind, a reduction in the number of livestock, an increase in the volume of tradesmen's bills unpaid, and the existence of alarming gangs of poachers and other depredators.[2]

The replies to the question on the relative state of arable and grass farming generally asserted the distress to be much greater on the former. Many declared, however, that the decline in the prices of meat, wool and dairy products would soon make the difference small.[3]

There was some difference of opinion expressed in the replies to the question respecting the currency situation. Much mischief, it was said, had been caused by the failure of country banks and some complained of low prices resulting from deflation. In Lincolnshire alone the diminution of country bank paper was estimated at £2½ millions and in

---

[1] *The Farmer's Magazine*, Vol. 17, p. 468.
[2] *Ibid.*, p. 468.   [3] *Ibid.*, p. 468.

Wiltshire it was stated to be £300,000, but there was no general agreement on this question.[1]

The letters on the state of the labouring class and the poor-rates give evidence of a great deal of unemployment and over a third of the replies describe the distress arising from the want of work as amounting to "great misery and wretchedness."[2] Some state that farmers who formerly contributed to the rates had become paupers themselves, throwing the whole burden on the landlords. Many complaints were registered that, "while the manufacturers, who have occasioned the chief burden, pay scarcely anything to the rates, the accumulated weight falls on the occupiers of land."[3] Many apprehensions were expressed that, if the system were continued, "it would, together with the tithes, absorb the total rental of the Kingdom, leaving nothing more to the landlords of it than that of acting as trustees and managers for the benefit of others."[4]

So many references have been, and will be, made to the burden which the poor-rates were to the landed classes that it seems worth while to stop here to note some statistics bearing on the problem. The following table shows that, although the purchasing power of the pound increased, the sums expended for poor-relief did not decline in proportion, an indication of an increase in the proportion of the population drawing on the funds.

[1] *The Farmer's Magazine*, Vol. 17, pp. 468-9.
[2] *Ibid.*, p. 469.   [3] *Ibid.*, p. 470.   [4] *Ibid.*, p. 470.

TABLE II

The Sums Expended for Poor Relief; Their Value in Wheat; and the Population of England and Wales, 1801–22 [1]

Year.	Sums Expended for Relief of Poor. £	Population of England and Wales.	Numbers of Quarters of Wheat for which the money could have been Exchanged.
1801	4,017,871	8,872,980	693,234
1803	4,077,891	9,148,314	1,428,751
1811	6,656,105	10,163,676	1,440,455
1814	6,294,581	10,775,034	1,746,474
1815	5,418,846	10,979,437	1,702,255
1816	5,724,839	11,160,557	1,503,240
1817	6,910,925	11,349,750	1,470,409
1818	7,870,801	11,524,389	1,881,466
1819	7,516,704	11,700,965	2,080,748
1820	7,330,256	11,893,155	2,226,913
1821	6,959,249	11,978,875	2,557,763
1822	6,358,702	12,313,810	2,940,440

Another complaint of the correspondents was the necessary payment of tithes. This practice, originated by the Church, had become an institution, but the right to collect the tithe from landowners in the parish did not remain entirely in the hands of the clergy. With the separation of Church and State in the reign of Henry VIII, some of these Church-rights were transferred to laymen. The difficulties connected with the tithes in kind had led to the commutation of some of them into money payments. This seems to have been the more common practice in the first quarter of the nineteenth century, but it was not until 1836 that the last remnants of payments in kind were swept away.

[1] Taken from Porter, G. R., *Progress of the Nation*, Vol. I, p. 82.

Tithe payments were a long-standing grievance of the landed classes. They tended to discourage improvements since the tithe recipients always shared in the benefits from them but never incurred any of the risks. In times of falling prices the payment of a fixed sum proved to be a heavy burden. It appears from the letters received by the Board that 10s. was paid per pound of rent in Dorsetshire and 9s. per acre for grassland in Berkshire.[1] No other estimates were given.

The last query of the Board dealt with possible remedies for the relief of the landed classes. The proposals listed below with the number of letters favouring each show that tax reduction was by far the most popular of all legislative relief measures.[2]

Remedies Suggested

1. The repeal or reduction of taxation	205
2. The reduction of rents	90
3. The commutation of tithes	47
4. Heavier duties on all agricultural produce	58
5. Bounties on the exports of corn	31
6. Increased paper circulation	21
7. To regulate the poor-rates, and especially by subjecting all property to bear its full share	34
8. Raise the price of corn, etc.	19
9. Establishment of corn rents	7
10. Repeal of the act for warehousing corn	12
11. Lending of Exchequer bills on good security	2
12. Continue the Bank Restriction	2
13. Encourage emigration	1
14. Reduce the interest on money	3

[1] *The Farmer's Magazine*, Vol. 17, p. 471.
[2] *Ibid.*, p. 471.

15. Establish public granaries, the corn to be purchased by the government . . . 8
16. Encourage distilleries 2
17. Government administration of the poor . 2
18. Repeal of the Corn Laws 1
19. Reduction of the quantity of land to be sown 2
20. Bounty on the cultivation of hemp . . 1
21. Remove tax on draining-brick . . . 1
22. Establishment of branch banks by Bank of England 1

The Board saw every evidence of a considerable decline in the future production of grain if these conditions presented by the letters continued for long.[1]

Some of the replies to the Board's letter bring out the distress of agriculture better than the general summary given. The following is from the letter of Wyrley Birch of Norfolk which was one of the most prosperous counties during the Wars.[2] It shows the difficulties of the landlords and tenants on arable land.

"I have one tenant on a tithe-free farm of 1,200 acres, honest and industrious, who has told me repeatedly that he could not go on. I have induced him to continue by not asking for any rent for two years and a half, and

---

[1] The Reporter for *The Farmer's Magazine* decided, after an examination of the correspondence printed with the conclusions of the Board of Agriculture, that "it is impossible to believe that the sentiments of the Board's correspondents have always been accurately reported." This difficulty was due primarily to the failure of the correspondents to answer the precise questions asked. But he says, "Enough, however, has been published to make out a case of general distress among all the several classes immediately dependent upon agriculture, to which it is universally admitted there has been no parallel for half a century at least."—*The Farmer's Magazine*, Vol. 17, Nov. 1816, p. 472.
[2] *Ibid.*, p. 473.

paying one-half year's property-tax for him. He has my promise not to ask him for more than £100 for the year ending at Michaelmas 1816, instead of £800. To another tenant I have promised his farm for nothing. Another tenant of mine, who is one year and a half in arrears of rent, is constantly telling me he should give up his farm of 1,250 acres; but it would ruin him to a certainty; his stock would not bring one-fourth of what it cost him. He must go on; and unless the price of corn rises immediately, must be ruined. It is ruin to sell farming stock now. From this cause, and from the patience of the landlords not collecting their rents, tenants have not generally given notice to quit. There is also an expectation that Parliament will do much to alleviate the distress of the farmers."

Another letter from Miles Bowker,[1] Dorsetshire, indicates the difficulties of those who had reclaimed land and made general improvements during the Wars.

"About four years ago, I had laid out in this quarter about £13,000 in rearing a flock of 1,000 Merinos, buying and improving 115 acres of life-hold, and otherways stocking, cropping, and improving 1,000 more acres of farming which sum is now by loss, and reduction of the value of stock, not less than half consumed; and if it was necessary to be brought to sale, would not bring as many crowns as it cost pounds, though it is notorious I can work arable much lower than the neighbouring farmer, whilst I have lived upon less than 1 per cent. of the capital. My boys, instead of being at school, are become labourers and ploughmen on the farms; and still, the more we do, only the more we lose; and though it is many weeks since I gave up my two farms, only one person hath yet appeared to look for either, and they do not appear likely to be let."

[1] *The Farmer's Magazine*, Vol. 17, Nov. 1816, pp. 475–6.

These letters present a gloomy picture in the case of both landlords and tenants. Farmers were no longer able to hire the best of men in some cases at unusually low wages. The result was that many of the agricultural labourers were unemployed and were forced to rely on the poor-rates for enough to keep alive.[1]

3. Legislative Relief, 1816

Most of the relief proposals suggested by the agriculturalists, as we have seen, called for some sort of legislative action on the part of Parliament. And, in view of the political strength of the landed classes, it was a foregone conclusion that the farmers' problems would become political issues. As it turned out, the major part of the session of 1816 was spent in discussing the agricultural situation.

Practically all of the speakers were agreed that there was a great deal of distress among the tenants and landlords as a result of the lower prices of both farm produce and farm property of all kinds. But they were not agreed as to the factors responsible for the decline in prices, or on the measures, if any, which Parliament should take to relieve the situation. The sharp differences of opinion on these matters are brought out in the summary of the discussion which follows.

The Chancellor of the Exchequer,[2] Mr. Vansittart,

---

[1] *The Farmer's Magazine*, Vol. 17, pp. 477–8.
[2] See Smart, Wm., *Economic Annals of the Nineteenth Century*, p. 514.

was inclined to blame those who delayed passage of the Corn Law in 1814 for a good share of the present distress. This delay, he said, allowed a large amount of foreign grain to enter the country in the latter part of 1813 and the first part of 1814. Together with the large crop of 1813, this importation caused the market to be greatly overstocked. Then, too, there were two more harvests which proved to be fully as good as average. These factors accounted, he thought, for a good share of the fall in agricultural prices, but the situation was also made worse by the fact that the Government, which had been spending £50 millions a year on army and navy supplies, began to curtail its orders. This affected the manufacturing as well as the landed classes. The distress of the latter would continue, he said, until all prices were lowered to the same extent as those of farm produce had been.

Mr. Western,[1] spokesman for the landed interests in the Commons, took a somewhat broader view of the situation. He agreed that the primary cause of the present distress was an oversupply of grain brought about by the harvests of 1813 and 1815 together with the large importations in 1814. That the fall in prices of grain could not have been due to any possible anticipation of peace was clearly proven, to his satisfaction, because it occurred between January and November of 1813. There were at that time, however, a number of contributing factors such as excessive taxation, the

[1] Smart, Wm., *op. cit.*, p. 515.

burden of the National Debt, the fluctuations in the paper circulation and the pressure of poor-rates and tithes, which made the situation worse. These burdens, he said, had easily been borne by the landed classes before 1813 but now that incomes had been greatly reduced they must have relief from the heaviest of them.

The great danger for the country under the circumstances was, he thought, that the oversupply would cause such a curtailment in production that there would be an alarming deficiency in the future. His remedy was for the government to remove the surplus then on the market. He did not seem to be just clear as to what was the best way of doing this. But he made two suggestions, one of which was that the government encourage individuals and companies to buy up grain to be stored "under the King's lock" by an advance of exchequer bills to the amount of one half the value of the grain purchased. The other suggestion was that the Government again pay a bounty on exports sufficient to cover the difference in costs of production of grain at home and abroad.

These measures would afford only partial relief. Agriculture must also be aided by higher prices for produce and land, and by tax reduction. The latter method he considered the most obvious and the most desired. Such taxes as those on barley, which included the taxes on malt, beer and spirits, making a total of £12,350,000 in all, the property tax, the tax on agricultural horses and the duty on hops were those which bore most heavily on the landed classes. A reduction in these would help, therefore, to relieve the distress.

The situation of the landed classes might have been much worse, he said, had it not been for the Corn Law of 1815. This measure had had the effect of keeping out further importations which would have meant still lower prices. But, he also pointed out, it had been definitely proven that the import price for grain did not necessarily set the minimum price in the home market.

This did not mean that he was satisfied with the protection which was afforded agriculture under the present laws. If protecting duties were placed on imports of rape, mustard, caraway, canary and clover seeds, the present situation would be improved because these could be grown on wheat lands. Tallow, cheese and butter were also being poured into the country from abroad, he said, and wool imports had increased from £7 millions to upwards of £15 millions. Higher duties should be placed on these articles, especially butter, for the Irish trade was being ruined by foreign competition.

It would be a mistake to suppose that Western's analysis was satisfactory to all the representatives of the landed classes in the Commons. Mr. Curwen [1] disagreed with him entirely about the large surplus of grain. There had never been one, he said, since 1792. An oversupply of grain could not, in any event, be the sole cause of the distress because the prices of all farm products had fallen. As a temporary measure, he proposed that the

[1] Smart, Wm., *op. cit.*, p. 522.

government make loans to farmers in cases where the landlord would give a half-year's rent as security for the loan. The interest on the loan could be paid jointly, 3 per cent. by the landlord and 2 per cent. by the tenant, and the principal would be payable in six, twelve or eighteen months.[1]

The speeches of Western and Curwen were reviewed along with the whole history of the situation in a long speech from Mr. Brougham, a Whig.[2] The distress, in his opinion, was due to the combined effects of overproduction and deflation. But the heavy taxes, particularly the poor-rates, added greatly to it. This tax, he pointed out, was unfairly distributed between the manufacturers and the agriculturalists, since the former were assessed only on the value of their real property regardless of the amount of income, while the landed classes were assessed on the full amount of the rental income.

Under the circumstances, those who had been speculating in land on savings, or borrowed money, could hope for no legislative relief measure. And, if the causes of the distress were largely overproduction and heavy taxes, it would be folly to grant a bounty on exports for it would tend to increase

[1] Under the Usury Laws, 5 per cent. was the maximum rate which the banks could charge. There was a considerable amount of agitation among the landed and other classes at that time for a revision of these laws because of the difficulty of obtaining loans. Banks had to maintain their reserves by refusing to discount paper of any kind, even the best, and farmers were driven to the money dealers who charged a high price for loans.
[2] See his speech as reported in Smart, Wm., *op. cit.*, pp. 526–34.

production and make the expenses of government still greater. To equalise costs of production with a bounty when the home price was 20s. higher than in foreign markets would cost, he said, a million pounds for every million quarters exported. Furthermore, the effect of exporting grain would be to raise the home price and make the system all the more costly.

The main sources of relief would have to be reductions in national taxation and the poor-rates. One way of bringing about the former would be, he suggested, to break into the Sinking Fund which had been accumulated to pay the principal on the public debt. As for a means of reducing the poor-rates, he considered Malthus' suggestion the only practical one. The latter's solution of the problem called for a withdrawal of all relief from the children of the present poor after they had reached a certain age.

Other suggestions for relief measures were: (1) a general upward revision of the Corn Laws; (2) the abolition of the warehousing system; (3) the removal of all restrictions governing the trade in wool; (4) the repeal of the laws forbidding tobacco to be grown in England; and (5) the repeal of the malt duties and a heavy import duty on butter. This last suggestion came from those especially interested in Ireland.[1]

The outcome of all this discussion was the appointment of a Select Committee to enquire into the feasibility of imposing a duty on foreign

[1] Smart, Wm., *op. cit.*, p. 521.

seeds.[1] It was also instructed to examine the operation of the laws on wool and woollen goods and the laws prohibiting the growth of tobacco in Great Britain.

The Committee found that no part of the distress seemed to have been caused by any inadequacy in the prices of wool and thought, therefore, that the laws respecting wool and woollen goods should not be changed.[2] It also did not understand how agriculture would benefit greatly from high protective duties on seeds. The Committee considered the English soil fit for growing tobacco but was reluctant to propose a change in the laws prohibiting its growth because of the loss in revenue to the Government.

Nothing came of the Committee's Report and, in the opinion of the Ministry, it was unnecessary to do more than had been done because the situation had already shown signs of improvement. Robinson,[3] Vice-President of the Board of Trade, and Lord Castlereagh,[4] Secretary of Foreign Affairs, both spoke against the various relief measures proposed. They made it plain that the Government was not in favour of giving more protection to agriculture.

The session, however, was not a total loss from the farmer's point of view. Three tax relief measures were passed which relieved the tax burdens of the landed classes considerably. The property tax, a tax of 10 per cent. on all incomes from funded

[1] Smart, *op. cit.*, p. 535.
[2] *Ibid.*, p. 536.
[3] *Ibid.*, p. 523.
[4] *Ibid.*, p. 534.

and landed property, except for those with relatively low amount of such property, was abolished. This meant a reduction of approximately £14 millions in revenue of which over £8 millions was paid by the landed classes. The tax on farm horses was reduced and the Chancellor of the Exchequer gave up the duties on malt which were a cause of complaint from the farmers.[1]

Before Parliament adjourned for the year, the prices of grain had begun to rise due, in the main, to the cold spring and wet summer both in Great Britain and on the Continent. The price of wheat doubled in 1816 between January and December, and the farmers seemed to consider the distress on the mend. In fact, it is reported that the rise in prices occasioned many applications for farms which had been abandoned by their former occupants.[2] The further fortunes of the landed classes will be taken up from this point in the next chapter.

[1] Smart, *op. cit.*, pp. 463–8. [2] *Ibid.*, p. 538.

CHAPTER IV

PARTIAL RECOVERY AND FURTHER DISTRESS, 1817–22

THE rise in the prices of grain which was noted in the previous chapter continued well into 1817. The price of wheat, which had reached 103s. 7d. in December 1816, maintained this high level until August 1817 and, after a sharp decline, rose again to 84s. by the end of the year.[1] Other grain prices behaved similarly to that of wheat. Consequently, the ports were open to foreign grain during practically all of the year and the excess of imports over exports of wheat and meal alone amounted to 1,020,949 quarters.[2]

Wheat did not sell at these high prices again in 1818, but in spite of the large excess of imports of wheat and meal over exports to the extent of 1,593,518 quarters, the price remained between 80s. and 90s. during the year.[3] This rise in the price of wheat from the low point of 52s. 10d., which it touched in January 1816, brought cheer to the landed classes.[4] But the large importations

---

[1] Tooke, T., *History of Prices*, Vol. II, p. 390.
[2] Porter, G. R., *Progress of the Nation*, Vol. I, p. 146.
[3] *Ibid.*, p. 146.   [4] Tooke, T., *op. cit.*, p. 390.

did not please them, and petitions asking for more protection were circulated among the English farmers.[1]

The general price level, according to the indices of Jevons and Silberling, rose about 12 per cent. over 1816 reaching a peak in 1818.[2] This rise in prices seems to have been followed by a partial recovery in general business conditions in the middle of 1817. In May of 1818 the Chancellor of the Exchequer reported an increase in the revenue at the rate of £100,000 a week and a generally satisfactory condition of the country.[3] Later in the year the Regent, in his speech closing the Parliamentary session, congratulated the country on its improved status and expressed every hope for a bright future.[4] An examination of the accuracy of his forecast will be deferred until a bit later in order to review some other events bearing on the progress of agriculture.

A significant development in the attitude of the country and the Government toward the system of protection was indicated in the session of 1817.[5] It was, in fact, an attack on the whole commercial policy which the Government had pursued for about two centuries. Brougham, first of all, called the attention of the members of the Commons to the depressed condition of practically all industries in 1815 and 1816. The contention made by the

---

[1] Smart, Wm., *Annals*, p. 654.
[2] See Silberling, N. J., *op. cit.*, *Review of Economic Statistics*, Vol. V, pp. 232 and 250.
[3] Smart, Wm., *op. cit.*, p. 652.   [4] *Ibid.*, p. 652.
[5] *Ibid.*, pp. 548–54.

Ministry that the distress was caused by the transition from war to peace was not satisfactory, he thought, as an explanation of such universal derangement. A more fundamental cause, in his estimation, was to be found in the Mercantilistic policy of the Government.

Such an attitude on his part, he admitted, might seem strange to the House since he had been a supporter of the Corn Law of 1815. This, however, was only a temporary measure passed under unusual circumstances, and was merely intended to give to agriculture that protection which had already been extended to manufacturing industries. There was, he contended, some justification for protective duties on grain but there was no excuse for high duties on timber, iron, copper, butter, cheese and French wine. Shutting off the imports of these goods had resulted in a curtailment of the demand for English manufactured products because trade was necessarily reciprocal.

An even worse blunder had been made in imposing a duty of 15 per cent. *ad valorem* on foreign linen which was only imported and then re-exported. This was, he pointed out, diametrically opposed to the principle of the Mercantilist School. The effect of trying to make consumers buy English manufactured linen, which they did not want, was the loss of the shipping trade in foreign linen.

There were other instances such as in the case of the trade in coal, wool and cotton in which restrictions had proven detrimental to the country's business. In fact, he declared, the whole commercial policy of the Government, including the Navigation Acts, had outlived its usefulness by a century. The blind pursuit of a restrictive policy had led to reprisals by other governments. English goods, in fact, were almost excluded from Russia, Prussia, Austria and the United States by retaliatory duties. The trade with Spain was in a worse condition than it had been before the Wars and it was clear, he thought, that England could expect little trade with France when there were still 130,000 British soldiers quartered on her soil.

This attack on the policy which the Ministry had pursued was answered by Robinson, Vice-President of the Board of Trade.[1] He admitted the validity of Brougham's major arguments but pointed out that the protective system was deeply entrenched. Now that a special case had been made of agriculture in 1815, the manufacturers, he said, would be likely to claim exceptional circumstances in their industries which would warrant higher protection. Unless both agriculturalists and manufacturers could be induced to give way, there could be no reciprocity in trade with foreign countries and this was as far as he carried the discussion at that time.

1. FURTHER DEPRESSION IN MANUFACTURING AND AGRICULTURE

The period of recovery proved to be short-lived. The general price level in 1819 fell back to about

[1] Smart, Wm., *Annals*, p. 604.

where it was in 1816 and the number of commissions in bankruptcy increased over 50 per cent. as compared with 1818.[1] The depression seemed to have been equally as great on the Continent and in the United States. Imports in 1819 declined over £6 millions and exports fell £9 millions as compared with the previous year.[2] These factors had a depressing effect on business and, as a consequence, there was a good deal of unemployment and discontent among the workers in the manufacturing industries.[3]

The agriculturalists also found their situation less prosperous in 1819. The price of wheat dropped below 80s. in February and the ports were closed to foreign wheat for the remainder of the year. This did not check the fall in its price, however, and by the end of the year wheat was selling at 66s. 3d.[4]

The landed classes gave notice at the beginning of the Parliamentary session that they were not satisfied with the Corn Law.[5] A large number of petitions were presented to the Commons stating that wheat could not be profitably grown in England at less than 80s. and inferred that the large importations in 1817 and 1818 were responsible for the decline in prices. They asked for the appoint-

[1] Taken from Silberling, N. J., *op. cit.*, *Review of Economic Statistics*, Vol. V, pp. 232 and 251.
[2] Smart, Wm., *Annals*, p. 690.
[3] This was the year of the famous " Peterloo Massacre " near Manchester. *Ibid.*, pp. 720-1.
[4] See Tooke, Thomas, *History of Prices*, Vol. II, p. 390.
[5] An account of the discussion on the petitions and the Corn Laws can be found in Smart, Wm., *Annals*, pp. 672-3.

ment of a Select Committee to consider the matter of putting agriculture on an equal basis with manufacturing with respect to protection. Their petitions made little headway with either the Ministry or the representatives of the landed classes in the Commons. It was almost universally agreed that an attempt to raise the protective prices on grain would meet with strong protests from the unemployed workers in manufacturing districts.

Far more important to the landed classes than the possibility of raising the import prices on grain was another measure passed by Parliament in the session of 1819. It will be recalled that the Ministry considered the resumption of specie payments by the Bank of England to be inexpedient in 1815 and the consent of Parliament to permit the continuance of the Restriction Act of 1797 was secured. Every year since the end of the Wars the question of suspending the Act had come up in the Commons only to have it deferred until some later date by the Ministry. But in 1819 both Houses appointed Secret Committees which were directed to enquire into the state of the Bank of England with a view to the resumption of specie payments and to take into consideration any other matters connected therewith. "Young Mr. Peel," then a man of thirty-one and a member for the University of Oxford, was appointed Chairman of the Commons Committee.[1]

On May 6 the Commons Committee made its

[1] Smart, Wm., *Annals*, pp. 673-4.

second report to the House.¹ Its examination of the financial condition of the Bank of England on January 30 showed that organization to have liabilities of £33,894,580 and assets of £39,096,900, leaving a capital and surplus of £5,202,320 exclusive of the Government's permanent indebtedness to the Bank of £14,686,800. The Committee agreed with the Directors of the Bank that the repayment of a large part of the loan made to the Government would be necessary before specie payments could be resumed. It therefore recommended to the House that £10 of the £19½ millions of the notes outstanding backed by Government securities be repaid immediately. This would give the Bank a great deal more control over the volume of its notes outstanding.

Although the Bank was in a sound financial position, the Committee deemed it inadvisable to revert to specie payments at the time fixed by law, July 5, 1819. Such a sudden reduction in the paper currency as it thought might be required would have disastrous effects on the business of the country. The Bank should, it argued, bring the value of paper back to a par with gold gradually. The Committee recommended, therefore, that, on a day to be fixed by Parliament, not later than February 1, 1820, the Bank be required to deliver

[1] A brief summary of the first Report which dealt with the attempts of the Bank to redeem part of its notes issued prior to January 1, 1817, can be found in Smart, Wm., *Annals*, pp. 675-6. The full text of the second report of Peel's Committee can be found in *Abstracts on Money and Prices in the United Kingdom*, Vol. II, in the Agricultural Economics and Farm Management Library of Cornell University.

gold bullion for notes at the rate of £4 1s. per ounce in amounts not less than 60 ounces. On or before October 1, 1820, the Bank should redeem its notes at the rate of £3 19s. 6d. an ounce and after May 1, 1821, it should deliver not less than 60 ounces at the old established price of £3 17s. 10½d. per troy ounce. This requirement to pay in gold should not extend for less than two, or more than three, years after May 1, 1821. At the end of this period cash payments should be resumed.[1]

This plan, in the estimation of the Committee, would enable the return to cash payments to be made more quickly than if the country's supply of gold were used for internal circulation. Gold would be used only to pay foreign trade balances and the Bank would, therefore, have a greater reserve of the precious metal.[2] It further suggested that the laws prohibiting the melting or exportation of gold coin be repealed.

The report of the Committee appointed by the Lords followed along the same lines as the report of the Commons' Committee.[3] There were long debates in both Houses on the question but Peel's Bill, embodying the recommendations of his Committee, was finally carried without alteration. The terms of this Bill provided that the payment of

[1] See the Report of the Committee in *Abstracts on Money and Prices in the United Kingdom*, Vol. II, p. 18.
[2] The Committee acknowledged indebtedness to Ricardo for this plan which is given in his " Proposals for an Economical and Secure Currency with Observations on the Profits of the Bank of England," which can be found in McCulloch, J. R., *The Works of David Ricardo*, pp. 391-437.
[3] Smart, Wm., *Annals*, p. 677.

notes in bullion be continued until May 1, 1823.¹ This exempted the Bank from providing at once a quantity of gold necessary to replace, in case the public should prefer coin to paper, all the smaller notes in circulation which the Lords' Committee estimated to amount to £15 or £16 millions.²

Although there was no statute regulating the amount of country bank notes which could be issued, they were limited, in the opinion of Mr. Ricardo and other " practical men " of that time, by the issues of the Bank of England.³ Consequently, it was expected that a reduction of the Bank's notes in circulation would be followed by a reduction in the paper money of country banks. Since no account was kept of the total amount of these notes in circulation, it is necessary to rely on the value of these notes stamped for circulation by the Government each year to get some idea of the changes in volume of this

[1] Smart, Wm., *Annals*, pp. 678–9.
[2] *Ibid.*, pp. 677–8.
[3] See Ricardo's discussion of the question in his " Reply to Mr. Bosanquet's Observations on the Report of the Bullion Committee " in *The Works of David Ricardo*, edited by J. R. McCulloch, 1886, pp. 348–53. He argues that the Bank of England notes were confined largely to the area about, and in, London and that the country bank notes did not circulate to any great distance from the emitting bank. Should the Bank of England increase its number of notes in circulation, prices in London would tend to rise. Consumers and other buyers there would ask for drafts on a country bank in return for notes in order to purchase in the cheapest market. This would tend to decrease the volume of Bank of England notes and, at the same time, the remittances from London to the country banks would permit them to increase their note issues. When a country bank made excessive note issues, economic forces working in the opposite direction brought higher prices in London and lower ones in the vicinity of the country bank.

part of the currency. The following table shows the effect of Peel's Bill on the total paper circulation of England.[1]

TABLE I

QUARTERLY AVERAGES OF BANK OF ENGLAND NOTES OUTSTANDING AND ONE-AND FIVE-POUND COUNTRY BANK-NOTES STAMPED, 1815-25

(Unit: 1 million pounds.)

Year.	Quarterly Averages Bank of England Notes in Circulation.				Quarterly Values One- and Five-Pound Country Bank-Notes Stamped.			
1815	27.3	27.0	27.2	26.1	12.4	9.7	9.0	9.0
1816	26.6	26.4	27.2	26.1	10.7	11.2	8.9	13.1
1817	27.1	27.5	29.5	28.9	14.6	14.4	17.7	22.3
1818	28.4	27.5	26.9	26.0	20.4	16.5	20.2	18.6
1819	25.8	25.4	25.5	23.9	11.1	6.4	6.8	7.2
1820	24.1	23.8	24.5	23.3	5.8	6.1	7.6	7.4
1821	24.2	22.9	20.7	18.5	7.6	7.2	9.5	10.5
1822	18.6	17.3	18.4	17.2	6.4	5.3	9.9	10.5
1823	18.1	18.0	19.3	19.1	7.3	7.7	9.4	8.9
1824	19.7	19.9	20.6	20.3	11.8	10.0	12.5	12.8
1825	21.1	19.8	19.8	19.7	13.3	16.1	17.3	12.8

It appears from the above table that both the Bank of England notes and the country bank notes contracted rapidly between 1818 and 1823. The former decreased about 30 per cent. and the value of the country bank notes stamped declined about 43 per cent. in this period. Both Jevons' and Silberling's indices of wholesale commodity prices show a decline of about 30 per cent. between 1818 and 1824.[2]

The data given by Tooke show that the market price of gold fell to the mint price in March 1820 and that the exchanges on Paris and Hamburg

[1] Taken from Silberling, N. J., *op. cit.*, *Review of Economic Statistics-Supplement*, Vol. V, pp. 255 and 258.
[2] *Ibid.*, p. 234.

came back to par at about the same time. It appears that the currency of the country was back on a gold basis in the early part of 1821, although it was then impossible to buy gold from the Government except in large quantities.

2. THE AGRICULTURAL DISTRESS, 1820

The downward trend in the price of wheat and other grain in 1819 continued with few interruptions throughout 1820. This meant, of course, that the ports were closed to practically all foreign grain by the operation of the Corn Law of 1815.[1] The farmers had expected this legislation to keep the prices of wheat and other grain at about the prices set for foreign imports; 80s. for wheat had come to be considered the average price and not that price which was just sufficient to meet the expenses of the high cost producers. Consequently, when they found that prices were falling in spite of the laws they again appealed to Parliament for relief.

A Committee representing the interests of the agriculturalists was sent to petition Robinson, President of the Board of Trade, for an upward revision of the Corn Laws.[2]

"The true standard of protection on all the productions of the soil [it argued] is the difference of expense

---

[1] See Tooke, Thomas, *op. cit.*, Vol. II, p. 390, for data on wheat prices.
Porter, G. R., gives the excess of imports of wheat and meal over exports for the year at 34,274 quarters, *op. cit.*, Vol. I, p. 146.
[2] See the Report of the Committee in *The Farmer's Magazine*, Vol. 21, Feb. 1820, p. 67.

at which all agricultural productions can be grown in foreign parts and in this country, and nothing short of countervailing duties equal in extent to this difference can protect the agriculture of this country."[1]

This difference in costs of production it estimated at from 25s. to 30s. the quarter on wheat and about 30 per cent. on all other agricultural products. The imports of foreign grain in the last six months had exceeded all former precedents, it said, and should the laws remain unaltered, the home growers would be ruined.

Neither Robinson, nor any of the other members of the Ministry, was prepared to take steps to alter the Corn Laws in the face of the unemployment among the manufacturing workers.[2] This did not prevent the landed classes from showering the Commons with petitions later in the session.[3] They demanded the same amount of protection for agriculture as had been given to manufacturing industries. A Select Committee, they said, should be appointed to consider the distress of the farmers and landlords which was the result of high poor-rates, excessive taxation, and inadequate protection.

The protectionists were told that agriculture was not as badly off as the petitioners claimed. In fact, of all the distressed classes, it was said, the landed interests had suffered least. What they really wanted was famine prices and bumper crops. It was evident, said Robinson, that there was no land which would not grow wheat if sufficient

---

[1] *The Farmer's Magazine*, Vol. 21, p. 68.   [2] *Ibid.*, p. 70.
[3] Smart, Wm., *Annals*, pp. 731-4.

capital were expended on it. He could not see that it was the duty of the legislature to keep poor land under cultivation when no Act had ever been passed calling it into use.[1]

In spite of the opposition of the Ministry, the motion for the appointment of a Committee was finally carried. But the importance of this victory was considerably minimised by the directions which Robinson succeeded in giving to it. His amendment instructed the Committee to

"confine their enquiry to the mode of ascertaining, returning and calculating the average prices of corn in the twelve maritime districts under the provisions of the existing Corn Laws, and to any frauds which might be committed in violation of any of the provisions of the said laws."[2]

The Committee reported to the House in July.[3] It had found the greatest neglect in making the proper returns on the amount and price of grain sold in every district except that controlled by the Corn Exchange, but it had no definite proof of any fraud in taking, or making, the returns to the receiver of grain returns in London. As far as it had been able to discover, there was no proof of any fraud connected with the warehousing system. The lateness of the session precluded discussion of the report, and nothing further seems to have come of it.

The session of 1820 was also notable for the petitions presented to Parliament by a different

[1] Smart, Wm., *Annals*, p. 733. [2] *Ibid.*, p. 734.
[3] See the report of the Committee in *The Farmer's Magazine*, Vol. 21, Nov. 3, 1820, pp. 389 ff.

H

class of people. Most of these were patterned after the one from the people of London which was presented to the Commons by Mr. Baring.[1] This petition called the attention of the House to the fact that the manufacturing industries had failed to recover appreciably from the depression of 1815-16 after nearly five years of peace. The remedy, it said, was to be found in the removal of many of the restrictions which had been placed on trade, especially the high protective duties on raw materials. Such a step would aid the manufacturers in two ways. In the first place, they would be able to get their raw materials cheaper, a factor which would enable them to undersell foreign competitors; secondly, greater importations of raw materials would increase the demand for English manufactured goods in foreign markets. The petitioners stated, however, that they had no desire to alter the Corn Laws at just that time.

Baring[2] was quite in agreement with the arguments advanced therein. He suggested the following changes in the commercial laws: (1) removal of the duty on foreign wool and the restrictions on the imports of timber; (2) abolition of the Navigation Acts; (3) removal of the duty on German linen; (4) alteration of the commercial relations with France; and (5) inauguration of free trade between India and England.

In the following debates the soundness of the principle of free trade was generally admitted but even the warmest supporters of this policy recog-

[1] Smart, Wm., *Annals*, pp. 744-59.   [2] *Ibid.*, pp. 747-8.

nised that its adoption would have to come slowly, if at all. There was the revenue to consider and, more important still, the interests of those people who had sunk capital into enterprises in the protected industries. An immediate withdrawal of the restrictions on trade would ruin many such investors.[1] The debates and the sentiment of the country show that 1820 may be taken as the year in which free trade began to be looked upon as a practical as well as an ideal policy.[2]

3. THE LANDED CLASSES AGAIN ASK FOR RELIEF, 1821-2

The prices of grain in 1821 continued at about the same level they had reached at the end of 1820. Wheat sold at about 54s. the quarter for the year, with the exception of the months of September and October.[3] The farmers became alarmed at the continuance of these relatively low prices and again petitioned Parliament for relief.

In the previous year, it will be recalled, the Ministry was adverse to the appointment of a Committee to hear the petitions of the landed classes. But the Tory party had been somewhat weakened by internal dissension since that time and, consequently, the Ministry felt the support of the petitioners to be more essential. This may have been the reason which led Robinson to endorse

---

[1] See a report of Ricardo's discussion in Smart, Wm., *Annals*, p. 748.
[2] *Ibid.*, p. 759.
[3] See Tooke, T., *History of Prices*, p. 390.

the motion for a Select Committee to investigate the distressed condition of agriculture.[1] At any rate, the Committee was duly appointed and instructed to examine the petitions and report to the Commons on the agricultural situation.

The Report of the Committee, which was presented in June and accepted as an able piece of work, was, nevertheless, a great disappointment to the landed classes. One of the correspondents of *The Farmer's Magazine* made the following comment on it:

"It is more like a chapter in a work on political economy than a report of the Committee of the House of Commons; and, it will either not be read by our farmers, or, if read, it will not be understood by these practical men, who are suffering from a powerfully depressing influence operating against them."[2]

The Ministry did not let the landed classes control the Committee by any means. As a matter of fact, the agriculturalists withdrew from its meetings in the hope that it would separate without reporting and, as a result, the free-traders on the Committee had it all their own way. This accounts for a large part of the antipathy of the landed classes toward the analysis of their situation which may have been able, but certainly was not helpful in the way they expected it might be.[3]

[1] See Hansard, S. 2, Vol. IV, pp. 1139–61.
[2] From "Some Remarks on the Report of the Select Committee on the Distressed State of Agriculture" in a letter to T. S. Gooch, Esq., M.P., from Simon Gray, Esq., printed in *The Farmer's Magazine*, Vol. 22, Aug. 31, 1821, p. 264.
[3] See Walpole, Spencer, *History of England*, Vol. II, p. 27.

The Report [1] covered four principal topics, namely: (1) the cause, or causes, of the distress; (2) the efficacy of the Corn Laws; (3) the prices of grain in foreign countries and the probable effects on English farmers of a system of free trade; and (4) the merits of the various relief measures proposed. Since this report played an important part in the subsequent discussion of relief measures, its recommendations and findings are briefly summarised.

(1) *The Cause, or Causes, of the Distress.*

The Committee considered the agricultural depressions in 1804 and 1814 similar to the present one. Both of the former situations were due, in the main, to a temporarily overstocked condition of the market and, therefore, both had proven ephemeral. The unusually large harvests of 1819 and 1820, especially the latter, accounted in a large part for the distress in 1821. But there was no doubt, it said, that the distress was due in part to the difficulties encountered in the transition from war to peace. The necessity of bringing the currency back to a gold standard basis, in particular, was responsible for some of the drop in the prices of grain.

It was disposed to agree with the statements of the agriculturalists about the great fall in profits and the difficulty of paying rents. Enough evidence

---

[1] The Report is printed verbatim but without the evidence presented by the various witnesses in *The Farmer's Magazine*, Vol. 22, 1821, pp. 325–44 and 387–410.

had been presented to convince the members that "the returns to an occupier of an arable farm, after allowing for interest on his investment, were by no means adequate to the charges and outgoings."[1] Both profits and rents had risen considerably during the Wars but, now that profits had fallen, there would have to be a readjustment of the contracts between tenants and landlords. The evidence, it thought, showed that tenants under long term leases had paid their rents with no more delay than usual under similar circumstances. In some cases, rents had already been lowered but this did not appear to have been general. The Committee expressed the hope that the farmers with the aid of rent reductions, savings and borrowings, would be able to weather the storm which would not last long.

In spite of the distress among the agriculturalists, the Committee found that the excise and custom returns from the principal articles of consumption showed a marked increase in the volume of trade within the last year, as compared with the preceding three years. The recovery of the cotton manufacturing industry from the depression which had begun in 1819 was notable. The exports of woollen goods, however, had declined. It was clear, thought the Committee, that agriculture had ailments of its own but the price level in America, the West Indies, and in the countries on the Continent of Europe, seemed to have fallen equally as much as the prices of grain in England. It was

[1] *The Farmer's Magazine*, Vol. 22, p. 326.

at a loss to explain this universal decline but thought that the state of foreign markets had affected domestic prices.

(2) *The Efficacy of the Corn Laws.*

Whatever was the cause of the distress, it could not be ascribed to inadequate protection. " Protection cannot be carried further than monopoly "[1] and this the home growers had been given since February 1819. No foreign grain, except for 700,000 quarters of oats in 1820, had come into the country since that time.

Although the Corn Laws afforded adequate protection when there was an average crop, both the farmers and the consumers were unduly injured by the operation of the laws. Wheat was not allowed to come into the country until the price reached 80s. and then there was no duty at all under the existing Corn Law. These regulations, the Committee thought, prevented consumers from having access to cheaper sources of supply and, in years of scarcity, occasioned unnecessarily high prices because of the difficulty of supplementing the home production from foreign sources. Once the ports were opened, they remained so for six weeks. This permitted large quantities of foreign grain to be dumped on the market which greatly depressed prices with great injury to farmers.

As a remedy for this situation, it suggested that all imports pay a fixed duty after wheat and other grain reached certain prices. These duties should be

[1] *The Farmer's Magazine*, Vol. 22, p. 338.

sufficient to equalise costs of production, including a fair profit to the domestic producer. In order to avoid giving any more protection than the present law afforded, it would be necessary to lower the import prices in accordance with the duties imposed. But the Committee was not prepared to say, at that time, what the new duties and prices should be.

(3) *The Prices of Grain in Foreign Countries and the Probable Effects on English Farmers of a System of Free Trade.*

The recommendations which the Committee made regarding the alteration of the Corn Laws were not to be put into effect immediately because of the glut in the grain markets on the Continent. If large quantities of foreign grain were admitted after the system of protection had been continued for so long, it would mean a great revulsion in agriculture. This was exactly the reason why the Committee also refrained from urging freedom of trade in grain. It appreciated the advantages of independence in time of war but expressed the opinion that no more restrictions than those absolutely necessary to prevent disaster should be placed on foreign imports.

(4) *The Merits of the Various Relief Measures Proposed.*

The remedy most often suggested in the petitions was tax reduction. The Committee entered into a theoretical discussion of the effect of taxes on profits. It pointed out that profits in agriculture had been as great during the Wars as those in the other industries. There could be no permanent difference in the rate in one industry, it said, because of competition. Those taxes which fell on agriculture in particular would increase the costs of production in this industry and could be shifted to consumers because the price of grain was determined by the expenditure for capital and labour necessary to raise such on no-rent land.

It did not consider the people of Great Britain, as a whole, overburdened with taxation as compared with other peoples when the *per capita* wealth of various nations was compared with theirs. But all taxes tended to bear heavily on a people when incomes were reduced and, therefore, the Government should reduce its expenditures as much as possible.

The agriculturalists claimed that in fairness they should be given the same amount of protection as was afforded manufacturing. This the Committee considered ill-advised for the following reasons. In the first place, it said, it is doubtful whether any manufacturing industry, with the exception of silk, derived any benefit under the existing duties. Proof for this statement was furnished by the fact that English manufacturers could undersell foreign producers in their own markets. In the second place, if profits in manufacturing industries were unusually large, they would be reduced by competition.

The suggestion that the Government abolish the warehousing system was quite futile, in the estimation of the Committee. It was obvious that grain could be brought from the Continent almost as quickly as it could be taken out of the warehouses and sent inland. The farmers, it thought, had no complaint on this score.

The possibility of alleviating the over-stocked condition of the home market by selling the grain abroad was thwarted by the presence of the same conditions on the Continent. Prices of grain were lower there than at home.

Was there nothing, then, that could be done to relieve the distress ? The Committee admitted that tenants under long leases were suffering severe financial embarrassment. Their position, it said, was made all the worse because of the slowness with which costs generally, and the wages of labour particularly, had responded to the changed value of money. But it concluded :

"So far as the present depression in the markets of agricultural produce is the effect of abundance from our own growth, the inconvenience arises from a cause which no legislative provision can alleviate ; so far as it is the result of the increased value of our money, it is one not peculiar to the farmer, but which has been and still is experienced by other classes of society." [1]

It confessed that after a long, tedious enquiry it could find no temporary measure, or modification of the existing laws, which would prove more of a help than a hindrance to the landed classes. Some readjustment to the lower prices, it noted, had already been made and in the continuance of this process lay the hope of the farmers.

Another Committee was appointed in 1822 which was instructed to review the findings of the previous

[1] From the Report in *The Farmer's Magazine*, Vol. 22, p. 409.

Committee and also hear the petitions which were presented.[1] This year the Ministry took the initiative in moving the investigation.

In order to give Parliament the opportunity to pass a relief measure during that session, the Committee made a preliminary report in April.[2] It did not attempt to give a complete, or adequate, explanation of the cause of the farmer's distress but the attention of the House was called to the fact that the amount of grain sold at Marklane between November 1, 1821, and March 1, 1822, exceeded the amount sold during the same period in the past twenty years.

Of the relief measures proposed, it considered two about equally futile. The first suggested that the bounty on exports be re-established. The possibility of exporting the surplus of grain even with the aid of a bounty, it said, was ruled out because of the low prices of grain on the Continent. The second impractical scheme proposed that the Government subsidise the farmers for a time by granting them loans on the security of the parish rates. Just why this was of no value the Committee did not say.

There were, however, two other suggestions deemed more worthy of consideration. The first provided that one million sterling of exchequer bills should be used by the Government to buy up a quantity of wheat and store it until the glut on the markets was relieved. Its stamp of disapproval

---

[1] Walpole, Spencer, *History of England*, Vol. II, p. 31.
[2] The report was reprinted in *The Farmer's Magazine*, Vol. 23, May 1822, pp. 152–60.

was put on this idea without any hesitation because it would put the Government into the grain business and set a dangerous precedent. The Committee refused to recommend it, therefore, even as a temporary measure.

The second proposal called for government loans to companies and individuals to encourage them to buy up grain and warehouse it for a time, in order that the total supply might be marketed in a more orderly fashion. Two different methods were suggested for putting this plan into operation. The first method provided that, when the price of wheat dropped under 58s. per quarter, a quantity not to exceed 600,000 quarters should be stored with the aid of a monthly allowance of 6d. per quarter from the Government until the price reached 65s. This loan should be paid in twelve or eighteen months. No single individual or company should be allowed to deposit more than a certain amount of wheat but the owners were to have the privilege of withdrawing their wheat at any time, providing all charges, including the loan, were paid.

The second method called for a loan from the Government of two-thirds of the market value of warehoused grain whenever the price of wheat was under 60s. Interest at 3 per cent. was to be paid on the loan. The period of deposit in warehouses should not exceed twelve months and the owner could withdraw his grain at will providing interest, warehouse rent, and the other charges, were paid. One million sterling would be enough to operate this plan successfully according to its proponents.

The Committee was inclined to favour this second method as a temporary measure but it was not completely satisfied with any of the proposals. It did suggest a remedy for the fluctuation in prices due to the Corn Laws which was in line with the suggestion in the report of the previous Committee. For wheat imports, a proper price would, it thought, be 70s. instead of the one in force which was 80s. Between 70s. and 80s. a duty of 12s. or 15s. should be imposed; between 80s. and 85s. it should be 5s. and above 85s., 1s. To prevent warehoused grain from being dumped on the market in excessive amounts, it suggested an additional duty of 5s. the quarter on such wheat during the first three months after the ports opened. The prices and duties on other grain should be adjusted in proportion to the changes made in those for wheat.

The Ministry favoured both the proposed revision in the Corn Law and the suggestion that £1,000,000 be set aside out of government funds to make loans on warehoused grain. The latter recommendation met its strongest opponent in Ricardo [1] and failed to pass the Commons. The proposed changes in the

[1] See Walpole, Spencer, *History of England*, Vol. II, pp. 31–2. Ricardo states his objection to the plan in his writings on "Protection to Agriculture" in McCulloch, J. R., *Works of David Ricardo*, 1886, pp. 486–7. His main argument was that, if the cause of the distress was "overproduction," the universal rule of allowing articles " to find their own natural level by leaving the supply to adjust itself to the demand " should be followed. If the low price of grain had been brought about by disorderly marketing, storing the surplus for a year, more or less, would merely put off the period of glut. Furthermore, the grain-dealers, through their speculative operations, would prevent prices from reaching excessively low levels with greater certainty than could the Government.

Corn Law were adopted without much opposition but it was provided that they should not come into operation until the ports were first opened under the law of 1815.[1] Since prices did not rise sufficiently to accomplish this between 1822 and 1828, when a new law was passed, the act was virtually a dead letter.

[1] A short summary of the Bill is given in Tooke, T., *History of Prices*, Vol. II, p. 36.

CHAPTER V

DEPRESSION AND RECOVERY, 1822-52

AT the end of 1822, over seven years had passed since the termination of the conflict with Napoleon and, as yet, agriculture had not recovered from the disastrous fall in prices which began in 1813 and 1814. The manufacturing and commercial industries were likewise in a depressed state during most of the six years following the Peace of Paris. But in 1821 both showed an improvement which was followed in succeeding years by a decisive recovery. The condition of the agriculturalists, however, improved more slowly. In most cases it is doubtful if there was any decided advance in English farming until after 1837, and it was not until the early years of the second half of the nineteenth century that agriculture experienced once again what might be called prosperous times. A number of questions naturally arise as to the reasons for this delay in readjustment and the causal factors which finally brought a turn of the tide. It is the purpose of this chapter to examine each of these phases of development.

1. THE EFFECTS OF THE FALL IN PRICES ON AGRICULTURE

The Committee,[1] appointed to hear the petitioners and investigate the condition of agriculture in 1821, called a great many witnesses from all parts of England, Scotland and Ireland representing not only the landed, but the trading and commercial classes as well. All subscribed to the statements of the farmers regarding the fall in the prices of farm produce, especially grain. But they disagreed as to the extent of the distress, its cause, or causes, and the measures, if any, which should be taken for the relief of agriculture.

The farmers unanimously voiced the opinion that the landed classes in all parts of the Kingdom were in dire straits and that they would be ruined in large numbers, unless something were done quickly to raise the prices of grain, or lower expenses in accordance with the present income from their produce. All agreed that wholesale prices had fallen to a much greater extent than retail, leaving the farmer with a smaller income with which to buy clothes, shoes, hats, etc. The wages of blacksmiths, carpenters, collar makers, wheel-wrights and agricultural labourers had also failed to come down in proportion to the fall of grain prices. Rents had been reduced somewhat, but not to the same extent as their incomes, and were paid, if at all, out of the farmer's capital rather than his profits. Some landlords had reduced their rents sufficiently to

---

[1] The report with minutes of evidence may be found in *Parliamentary Papers*, Vol. 9.

keep their tenants and it was generally agreed that this was a much wiser policy than that of clinging to the old rates—a course which must result in the failure of the tenants. Taxes, likewise, were paid out of capital or borrowed money, and they complained loudly against the tithe and high poor-rates. It was true, they said, that taxes had been reduced but, when the present rates were compared with those of the war period reduced to gold prices, it would be seen that, as a matter of fact, taxes were really higher now than before.

The distress, according to the farmers, was greatest on arable land. Grain prices had fallen more than those of meat and wool and, consequently, the very branch of agriculture which had received the greatest stimulus during the Wars was now the hardest hit. Those who had borrowed money to reclaim waste, or to improve the heavy clay lands, were past all relief, for it was the poorest arable lands which were bound to be thrown out of cultivation by the fall in prices. The distress was by no means confined to these relatively few farmers, since land values in general had been cut in half and, in some cases, no one could be found who was willing to take farms even as a gift because of the heavy taxes. Landlords, who had burdened their estates with mortgages and had little capital with which to withstand the financial strain, were finding themselves in " a universal march of ruin." The current situation was aggravated by the failures and losses incurred in 1815–16 from which farmers and landlords had not yet recovered.

It was generally agreed that, on an average of years, the country had been able to supply sufficient grain to satisfy the domestic demand. But the farmers were of an opinion that this would not continue to be the case unless something were done to relieve the distress. Under existing circumstances, improvements and repairs would be curtailed, stock would have to be sold to pay debts, and a large amount of land would be forced out of cultivation. The result was bound to be a considerable reduction in production. Other witnesses thought that the rapid strides toward more scientific cultivation, along with other improvements in agricultural machinery, methods of draining, etc., would offset the loss of some land.

When the witnesses were asked why tenants did not leave farms when conditions were so adverse, the Committee was told that a great many had already done so, especially those who had held land on short term leases. Some were holding on because they expected Parliament to do something for them. Those who had leased land for a relatively long period of time had spent a great deal of their income in making improvements on their farms, and this was a great inducement for them to continue and hope for the best. Another powerful deterrent to quitting the agricultural industry, the witnesses said, was the low price of stock and land; it meant ruin to sell at the prices then being offered. This accounted for the failure of many yeomen who were forced to sell their stock to pay taxes. The wealthy landlords could more easily stand the financial strain and were taking advantage of the unfortunate situation of these small farmers by acquiring good land at low prices.

Most of the people examined by the Committee considered that the wage-earners' situation had greatly improved because of the fact that wages had not fallen to the same extent as had the prices of grain. They admitted, at the same time, that there was more unemployment among the agricultural labourers, since farmers could not afford to maintain their former wage outlays. It was well known, they said, that the city workers who were working full time were much better situated than they had been during the Wars.

As to the causes of the fall in prices, most of the farmers and landlords were inclined to attribute the major part of their troubles to Peel's Act of 1819 which, they said, had operated to reduce the amount of currency in circulation. Some were inclined to blame the Corn Laws because they had permitted the large importations of 1817 and 1818. These large supplies of foreign grain had precipitated the fall in prices which were later depressed because of both deflation and overstocked markets, according to this view.

Another explanation decidedly contrary to that holding the alterations in the currency responsible for the distress was given to the Committee by Thomas Tooke.[1] He argued that the prices of grain were bound to fluctuate a great deal from year to year because both the demand and the

[1] *Parliamentary Papers*, Vol. 9, p. 224.

supply were relatively inelastic. Reference to past experience showed, he said, that farmers received, in general, a larger net income from a small crop of good quality than they did from an unusually large one equally good. If an ordinary harvest satisfied the home demand for grain, prices must fall considerably before the surplus would be taken off the market. In the light of this analysis, he maintained that the large importations of 1817 and 1818, in addition to the unusually abundant harvests of 1820 and 1821, were quite sufficient to account for the fall in the prices of grain. The decline in the prices of manufactured goods was the result of the overtrading in these products during the prosperous years of 1817 and 1818. At any rate, and about this point he was very positive, no more than 5 or 6 per cent. of the fall in the prices of all commodities could be ascribed to deflation, since the difference between the mint and market prices of gold was no greater than this amount when Peel's Bill was enacted in 1819. This view, as we have seen, was also held by Ricardo who served as a member of the Committee.[1]

2. Western's Scheme for Relieving the Distress, 1822

There were some members among the representatives of the landed classes in Parliament who were convinced that an increase in the currency would

[1] For Ricardo's views on the agricultural depression and the various remedies proposed see his work "On Protection to Agriculture" in *The Works of David Ricardo*, edited by J. R. McCulloch, 1886.

be necessary to restore profitable prices for agricultural produce. Another radical suggestion was made by Sir Francis Burdett,[1] the member for Westminster. He boldly demanded a readjustment of the public burdens on the ground that " the man who had lent his money when Bank paper was legal tender had no right to expect that he should be paid in gold." [2]

Western,[3] member for Essex and spokesman for the landed interests, favoured Burdett's proposal but he wished to go about reducing the burden of the debt somewhat differently. He was not in favour of paying the public creditor £3 instead of £4, but he did urge that the purchasing power of £4 be reduced to what £3 then represented. This was justified, he argued, because at the time the debt was contracted wheat sold at 80s. the quarter, or more; it would be only fair to the landed classes that the price of wheat should be brought back to 80s. when the debt had to be paid. Grain, not gold, should be made the standard of value.

Both Burdett's and Western's suggestions were defeated for the time by William Huskisson who made a strong speech supporting the gold standard.[4] But Western would not accept one rejection as final. He kept on agitating for a change in the currency laws and before the session was over a bill was passed suspending the redemption of the £1 and £2 notes of the country banks until 1833, when

---
[1] Walpole, Spencer, *History of England*, Vol. II, p. 32.
[2] *Ibid.*, p. 32.
[3] *Ibid.*, pp. 32–3.   [4] *Ibid.*, pp. 33–4.

the charter of the Bank of England would expire.[1] As the law stood previous to 1822, these notes were to be retired in 1823 when the Bank of England resumed cash payments. The representatives of the landed classes were inclined to regard this measure as a mild form of farm relief in so far as it would lead to inflation.[2] Since the notes of the country banks were to have been made payable in gold, they thought that the postponement of gold payments would help a great deal toward raising prices. The Prime Minister [3] denied that it was the intention of the Government to pass any such law as a remedy for the agricultural distress. In fact, he expressed strong opposition to decreasing the value of money as a means of reducing the National Debt.

3. THE CRASH OF 1825-26

It is a difficult matter to draw any definite conclusion as to the effects of the Act, which has just been considered, on either agricultural or non-agricultural prices. The general price level, according to the indices of Jevons' and Silberling, rose slightly in 1824 and 1825,[4] dropped back again in 1826, and then continued to fall until 1830. There were, however, a number of complicated economic

---

[1] Turner, B. B., *Chronicles of the Bank of England*, p. 114.

[2] See the debates in Hansard, 2nd Series, Vol. 7, 1822, pp. 150 ff., 877 ff., 928 ff., 1521 ff. and 1596 ff. This reference is to the debate in the House of Lords on the third reading of the " Small Notes Bill," pp. 1661-4.

[3] *Ibid.*, pp. 1663-4.

[4] Silberling, N. J., *op. cit.*, *Review of Economic Statistics Supplement*, Vol. 5, p. 234.

forces acting on prices between 1822 and 1826 which makes an estimate of the effect of any one particularly hazardous.

It is clear that the prices of meat and grain rose in 1824 and 1825, although those of wool actually fell.[1] The rise in non-agricultural prices was due in part, at least, to the wave of speculative buying which swept over the country. This speculation was confined at first to those goods which were ordinarily sold in Mexico and South America but it gradually spread to other commodities as prices rose. Many companies were organised to trade with these countries and the financial side of the boom resembled the operations involved in the famous South Sea Bubble which had burst over a century before.[2]

Confidence in the new financial organisations and the continued rise of prices began to wane toward the end of 1825 and, by December of that year, the country was on the verge of an acute financial crisis. The consequent rapid fall in prices caused the failure of several large banks and thirty-six country banks. Even the Bank of England had a narrow escape from having to resort to another Restriction Act. It is said that the country bankers greatly extended their issues of small notes between 1823 and 1825, thereby contributing to the rise in prices and the ensuing distress.[3] This opinion is borne out by the data given by Silberling on the value of country bank notes stamped which shows

[1] Driver, G. N., *Journal of the Statistical Society*, Vol. 1, p. 56.
[2] Andréadès, A., *History of the Bank of England*, pp. 248–55.
[3] Turner, B. B., *Chronicles of the Bank of England*, pp. 114–15 and 118–23.

that this part of the currency must have more than doubled between 1822 and the end of 1825.[1]

This crisis led to the passage of a bill by Parliament in 1826 which reorganised the country bank system. It permitted joint-stock banks having any number of partners to be established 65 miles or more from London, and gave them the power to issue notes. At the same time, bank notes of values less than £5 were abolished. This forced the Bank of England to redeem between £7 and £8 millions of notes.[2]

In spite of the crash of 1825 and the subsequent fall in the general price level, prices of grain were sustained at nearly their 1824–5 level in 1826 and 1827 by poor harvests. This caused a great deal of opposition to the Corn Laws among the unemployed manufacturing workers and they demanded that Parliament alter the restrictions on grain imports so as to give them cheaper bread. Although the Ministry did not have a great deal of sympathy for this class of people, it felt compelled to do something about the situation for political reasons.

4. CORN LAW REVISION, 1826–8

Rioting and incendiarism broke out among the unemployed manufacturing workers in the spring and summer of 1826. In Manchester troops had to be called out to quell the disturbances; the soldiers were forced to fire on the mobs to check them.

---

[1] Silberling, N. J., *op. cit.*, Review of Economic Statistics Supplement, Vol. 5, p. 258.

[2] Andréadès, A., *History of the Bank of England*, pp. 254–5.

FARM RELIEF IN ENGLAND, 1813–1852

These workers attributed their distress to the operation of the Corn Laws and, whether they were right or not, the Ministry felt compelled to take some action, the country being on the eve of a General Election.[1]

It proposed that the grain held in bond under the warehouse system be admitted into the country to relieve the situation. Wheat, at that time, was selling at about 60s. per quarter and the price would have to rise to 80s. before imports would be admitted under the existing law. The agriculturalists in the Commons objected strongly to the measure but it was finally carried with the stipulation that the bonded grain pay a duty of 12s. per quarter.[2] About 300,000 quarters of wheat, a relatively insignificant amount, was admitted under this Act. Shortly afterward provision was made for the admission, at the discretion of the Ministry, of imports of foreign wheat, up to 500,000 quarters, duty free.

The following year the Ministry proposed a bill modifying the Corn Laws based on the principle of a sliding scale which Huskisson, the originator of the idea, had previously suggested in the debates on the Bill of 1815. The purpose of the measure was to stabilise the price of grain, all kinds of which were to be capable of importations at any time on payment of the duties. These were to vary with the price of grain, decreasing as the price rose and increasing when it fell; the increase or decrease to be double the change in price beginning with

---

[1] Walpole, Spencer, *History of England*, Vol. II, pp. 141–2.
[2] *Ibid.*, p. 143.

20s. per quarter when wheat was at 60s. Other duties and prices were adjusted in like proportion to the change in the price of wheat.[1]

The agriculturalists were unanimously opposed to the Bill. It would afford inadequate protection, they said, because the British farmer could not raise wheat profitably at a price of 60s. per quarter. This opposition, with the aid of inaction and indecision on the part of the Ministry, succeeded in protracting the debates on the Bill through the session of 1827 and well into the session of 1828.

The Cabinet[2] met three times during March 1828 without coming to any agreement as to what should be done about the proposed Bill. Huskisson finally suggested a compromise which, with a slight modification, was finally accepted by the Cabinet and both Houses of Parliament. He proposed that the 20s. duty on wheat should commence when the price was at 60s. but, if more than 200,000 quarters of grain were imported in any twelve weeks, the duty should increase by one-fourth until the average price amounted to 66s. In order to appease some members of the Cabinet, this latter suggestion was amended to read one-fifth instead of one-fourth and, with this modification, a new Corn Law was framed and passed not, however, without a near rupture in the Ministry.[3]

[1] Walpole, Spencer, *History of England*, Vol. II, pp. 436-7.
[2] *Ibid.*, pp. 477-8. [3] *Ibid.*, pp. 477-8.

5. THE FARMERS AGAIN PETITION PARLIAMENT

The effects of the crash of 1825 on manufacturing, commerce and agriculture were anything but beneficial. The testimony of various members of the Commons in 1829 was uniformly gloomy. Agriculture appears to have suffered equally with other classes in spite of the fact that poor harvests in 1828, 1829 and 1830 helped to keep the price of wheat above 60s. The representatives of the landed classes were determined not to let the country forget the unfortunate circumstances of the farmers and agricultural labourers. The large farmer, they said, was reduced to a small farmer, the small farmer was becoming a labourer and the labourer was becoming a pauper.[1] The unemployed workers in all trades were thrown on the poor rates and thus the expense of their maintenance was passed on to the landed classes.

In 1822, the agriculturalists were strongly enough represented in Parliament to force a reluctant Ministry to accede to their demands for a Select Committee to investigate the agricultural distress. But in 1832-3, when they again pressed their claims for a hearing, the political situation had become still more adverse. A gradual weakening of the Tory party had been in progress and —more important—the Reform Bill of 1832 had reapportioned the seats in the Commons so as to give a larger representation to the manufacturing classes. Certain other reforms, such as the abolition of " rotten boroughs," and a relaxation in the

[1] Walpole, *op. cit.*, pp. 530-1.

requirements for voting, tended to make this Parliament a more democratic one than that which had lent a sympathetic hand in 1815.[1] Although the Whigs had a substantial majority, they were not united behind their Ministry and, consequently, the landed class representatives with the help of the "radical reformers" formed a formidable block of opposition. This combination of circumstances enabled the agriculturalists to secure the appointment of a Select Committee directed "to enquire into the present State of Agriculture and of Persons Employed in Agriculture in the United Kingdom."[2]

This Committee found that the farmers were no better off than in 1821, in that the incomes on farming capital were still below what was considered a fair return. It was true, it said, that some of the burdensome taxes had been reduced, or removed, since then but it pointed out that local taxes, such as the poor-rate and county-rates, had been increased.

The Committee of 1821 had expressed the hope that the savings of farmers, or perhaps temporary loans, would enable them to weather the storm until things should become readjusted. It now seemed to the investigators, from the evidence presented to them, that the savings of farmers, if there had been any, were all gone, or were greatly diminished. Credit, they said, was difficult to obtain and the resources of farmers were exhausted.

[1] Cross, A. L., *A Shorter History of England and Greater Britain*, Chapter 50, especially pp. 653-4.

For the Report of the Committee see *Parliamentary Papers*, Vol. 5, Session 1833.

The difficulties of the agriculturalists during the past twelve years had resulted, according to the report, in the abandonment of a considerable acreage of cultivated land. Improvements had been postponed; buildings had deteriorated; and farmers had attempted to get everything possible from the land without putting much back into it. A consideration of these facts, along with an examination of the stocks of grain on hand at that time and the amount of imports since 1821, led the Committee to conclude that: (1) the grain grown in Great Britain on an average was insufficient to supply the home demand; (2) the increasing amounts of grain which had been coming from Ireland were not sufficient to cover the deficiency; and (3) the United Kingdom was necessarily forced to rely on a supply of grain from foreign countries, even in years of average crops.

The farmers of Ireland, it found, had benefited by the increasing demand for grain in England. Production there was increasing and the distress did not seem as great. Some of the evidence given by witnesses also showed a much less serious situation in Scotland where rents were paid in kind more often than in money.[1] But the distress everywhere was greater on arable land than on grass lands, mainly, it thought, because meat prices had declined less than those of grain.

The Committee found that landlords in every part of the Kingdom, though in varying degrees, had reduced rents, except in cases where they had

[1] *Parliamentary Papers*, Vol. 5, Session 1833, p. 9.

not been raised during the Wars, or where the soil had been permanently improved by applications of capital. This almost universal reduction in the income of the owners of estates, the Committee said, caused considerable financial embarrassment, especially in the case of those who had heavily burdened their lands with mortgages and family settlements. In fact, according to the report, the depression had already resulted in an extensive transfer of ownership of land from the small, and financially weak, owners to the wealthy landlords.

One development of a more optimistic nature pointed out by the Committee was that some farmers had at least partially sustained their profits by self-help. A better rotation of crops, more extensive use of manures and facilities for draining land, and the application of science in breeding sheep and cattle were the factors which had contributed to the success of these comparatively few. A more extensive practice of these principles of scientific farming, it intimated, would help to solve some of the farmers' financial troubles.

The main cause of the distress, the report said, was to be found in the alterations made in the currency as a result of Peel's Bill of 1819. This measure had brought about a great reduction in the farmer's income but his expenses, including wages, rents and taxes had not dropped proportionately. Although Parliament could not legislate to restore the proper proportion in all of these outlays, it could help, suggested the report, in the following ways: (1) pass a law providing for the permanent commutation of tithes; (2) revise the poor-laws so as to do away with the evils of out-door relief; (3) repeal the law of settlement which prevented the free movement of labourers from one parish to another.

This, however, was as far as the Committee went in recommending legislative relief measures. "The legislature," it said, "can do much evil, but little positive good, by frequent interference with the agricultural industry." [1]

Although the report presented a gloomy picture of the condition of the landed classes in general, it stated a belief that, in spite of the unemployment, the agricultural workers in 1833 were better off than they had been during the Wars. The reason for their higher standard of living was that the purchasing power of money had increased without a proportionate decline in nominal wages.

6. SOME OBSERVATIONS ON THE REPORT OF 1833

The conclusions which the Committee reached, as a result of its investigation of the condition of agriculture in 1833, were subjected to considerable criticism by an economic historian, Mr. G. R. Porter, who published an account of the progress of agriculture in 1836.[2]

"The appointment of the Committee of 1833 [he said] was a concession made to those members of the House of Commons who fancied themselves interested in the continuance of the present system of Corn Laws

[1] *Parliamentary Papers*, Vol. 5, Session 1833, p. 3.
[2] Porter, G. R., *Progress of the Nation*, Vol. I, pp. 143–86.

and, accordingly, the whole tendency of the evidence given appears to make out the existence of distress among agriculturalists, the amount of which would be aggravated by any alteration of the law." [1]

In his estimation the evidence applied mainly to the condition of farmers on the poorest land and, therefore, was no indication of conditions in general.

It was true, he conceded, that war-time rents had not been maintained; but this was no proof that the landlords were worse off than before the Wars. He found that rents, in general, had at least doubled in every part of Great Britain since 1790 and inferred that, if the situation of the landlords had not improved, it could be attributed to their own carelessness or miscalculation. [2]

He also disagreed with the Committee's statement to the effect that the country was no longer self-sufficient. In fact, his data showed that the trend was toward less, rather than greater, dependence on foreign supplies. The witnesses had presented a picture of run-down lands and ill-kept buildings but he found evidence to show that the amount of capital invested in land had not decreased. [3] And in spite of the distress, there was actually more land under tillage in 1836 than there was in 1814. [4]

Proof that the country had not yet been forced to rely on foreign supplies of grain to any great extent was afforded by a statement of the excess of wheat and meal imports over exports since 1800. [5] The annual average importation for the decade

[1] Porter, G. R., op. cit., p. 163.   [2] Ibid., p. 164.
[3] Ibid., p. 167.   [4] Ibid., pp. 161–2.   [5] Ibid., p. 156.

1811–20 was 458,578 quarters. It increased between 1821–30 to 534,927 quarters, mainly because of two unusually deficient crops in 1829 and 1830. But the average for the first five years of the decade 1831–40 showed a decline to 398,509 quarters. This remarkable development, he thought, indicated a great increase in production and called for some explanation, since it occurred in the presence of a severe agricultural depression.

There were three possible explanations which he considered. One was that the area under cultivation had greatly expanded. An examination of the probable increase in the acreage brought under cultivation by enclosure since 1820 showed that only about 400,000 acres had been added in this manner and he considered such a small increase relatively unimportant.[1]

Statistics on the growth of population and its division into occupational classes showed, to his satisfaction, that the larger production could not have come from a greater number of farmers and farm labourers. In fact, the number of families dependent on agriculture had increased only $7\frac{1}{4}$ per cent. between 1811 and 1831, while the total number of families in 1831 was 34 per cent. larger than in 1811.[2]

Finally, there was the possibility of larger home production resulting from improvements in farming methods to be considered. There had been a good deal of progress made in this direction during

[1] Porter, G. R., *Progress of the Nation*, Vol. I, p. 171.
[2] *Ibid.*, p. 148.

the first quarter of the century, he found, owing to the activities of the Board of Agriculture and the investigations of progressive farmers. The fall in prices had also brought pressure on the agriculturalists to lower costs and virtually forced them to take up improvements. These facts explained why it was that 10,000 acres of arable and pasture land in 1831 supported 5,555 people, while in 1801 the same area provided for only 4,327.[1] Should production continue at this rate of increase, Great Britain would be able to supply her own food for quite some time. There was a possibility that the rate might even be accelerated, he thought, since the improved methods were not widely practised.

7. Poor-Law Revision, 1834

Before the Select Committee on Agriculture made its report to the House of Commons in 1833, another Committee had been appointed to consider one of the long-standing grievances of the farmers and landlords, namely, the administration of the poor-laws. Probably the recommendation of the Agricultural Committee respecting these laws had something to do with the consideration which the Commons gave the suggestions of the Poor-Law Committee when it reported in 1834.[2]

It was an able report and the changes in the laws which it suggested received careful attention before being enacted into law. The main objects

---

[1] Porter, *op. cit.*, p. 150.
[2] Taken from Cross, A. L., *A Shorter History of England and Greater Britain*, pp. 657–8.

FARM RELIEF IN ENGLAND, 1813-1852

of this legislation were to eliminate outdoor relief and to assure a better adjustment between the demand for and the supply of labour in the future so as to prevent unemployment. Although the immediate effect of the measure was to produce some suffering, it brought a reduction in the rates and a more wholesome condition among the poorer class of labourers. Some idea of the expense of maintenance of the poor under the old system, as compared with the first few years under the new law, is given by the following table.[1]

TABLE I
TOTAL SUMS ASSESSED AND LEVIED FOR POOR RELIEF

Year.	Total Sums Assessed and Levied. £	Year.	Total Sums Assessed and Levied. £
1803	5,348,204	1826-7	7,784,352
1812-13	8,640,842	1828-9	7,642,171
1814-15	7,457,676	1830-1	8,279,217
1816-17	8,128,418	1832-3	8,606,501
1818-19	8,932,185	1834-5	7,373,807
1820-1	8,411,893	1836-7	5,294,566
1822-3	6,898,153	1838-40	5,613,938
1824-5	6,972,323		

8. THE TITHE COMMUTATION ACT OF 1836 AND OTHER TAX REDUCTION MEASURES

Two years after the Poor Law was revised, another Act was passed by Parliament which aimed to propitiate a long-standing grievance of the farmers.

[1] Taken from Porter, G. R., *Progress of the Nation*, Vol. II, p. 357.
The figure for 1838-40 is from McCulloch, J. R., *The British Empire*, Vol. II, p. 669.

This was the Tithe Commutation Act which provided for the substitution of variable money payments for tithes in kind. The money payments were to be adjusted periodically for changes in the prices of farm produce so as to give the tithe owners a fixed amount of purchasing power. Both the farmers and the receivers of tithes stood to benefit from this measure; the former would have their payments reduced when prices fell and the latter would be paid more when prices rose. It seems quite probable that this definite settlement of the contractual obligations of the farmers contributed to the recovery of agriculture.[1]

Both the poor-rates and the tithes were local charges against the farmer's income. It remains to be seen what was done after the Wars to reduce the national taxes. The decennial averages of the total National revenues from all sources, and the amount paid *per capita*, is shown by the following table.[2]

TABLE II

A COMPARISON OF TOTAL AND *Per Capita* NATIONAL TAXES BY DECADES, 1801–1850

Years.	Total National Taxes Paid. £	Amount per Head of Population. £ s. d.
1801–10	57,273,820	5 12 2
1811–20	74,556,411	3 15 6
1821–30	58,637,645	2 12 9
1831–40	51,171,619	2 0 5
1841–50	55,542,842	2 0 11

[1] Lord Ernle, *English Farming Past and Present*, pp. 343–5.
[2] Taken from McCulloch, J. R., *The British Empire*, Vol. II, Appendix, p. 23.

It will be noted that, although the totals paid did not decrease appreciably in the last three decades as compared with the first two, *per capita* taxation after 1821 was reduced to about half the average paid in the period 1801–10. But the fact that the purchasing power of money about doubled between the first and last decades should be kept in mind when considering the real amount of the reduction.

9. Legislative Relief asked for Again

The distress among the landed classes, which the Select Committee of 1833 had been appointed to consider, was intensified by another period of falling prices. Wheat, which sold for 67s. 10d. the quarter in 1831, brought only 36s. 1d. in 1836.[1] Out of force of habit, the agriculturalists petitioned Parliament again for relief.

For the fifth time within a period of sixteen years, the Commons appointed a Select Committee to hear the petitioners and investigate the agricultural situation.[2] There were thirty-three members appointed to serve and, since most of them were representatives of the landed classes, there could be no question that the farmers would receive fair treatment.

Two reports were made to the House in 1836.[3] These stated that the fall in prices was due mainly to the abundant harvests since 1833 but that the

[1] Tooke, Thomas, *History of Prices*, Vol. II, p. 390.
[2] Walpole, Spencer, *History of England*, Vol. III, p. 372.
[3] See *Parliamentary Papers*, Session 1836, Vol. 8, Part I.

retirement of small bank notes after 1826 had tended to depress prices in general. This decline in prices had caused the occupiers and owners of the heavy clay lands the most suffering. In those districts where this type of land was common, tenants had become insolvent and, as a consequence, rents, poor-rates and tradesmen's bills were unpaid.[1]

The remedies which were suggested by the Petitioners were: (1) reduce the county taxation rates; (2) grant permission to the distilleries to use wheat and barley; and (3) secure farmers ready loans at low interest rates. The Committee could agree on no recommendation to be made to the House and merely submitted a report of their findings. It told the farmers plainly enough, however, that they would have to look to their landlords for relief rather than to any parliamentary measure. Consequently, the whole investigation was a complete failure from the point of view of the landed classes.

10. Preparations for General "High Farming"

We have seen that the House of Commons gave the landed classes a Select Committee to investigate their distress on the average of about every five years between 1813 and 1837. It is only fair now to ask what they did to help themselves during this period.

Although Porter's data on the growth of production in the United Kingdom between 1800 and 1836 shows a considerable gain from improvements in cultivation, he admits that such progress was

[1] See *Parliamentary Papers*, Session 1836, Vol. 8, Part I, p. 91.

not general.¹ Scientific principles were more generally practised by the farmers on grass lands than in arable farming and, consequently, those farmers who specialised in cattle and sheep raising had weathered the depression more easily.

On arable lands the open-field system was still extensively practised and farms were as yet relatively small. Little land had been drained and manure and artificial fertilisers were used by relatively few farmers. Cattle were still housed in draughty buildings under conditions which encouraged disease. Farm machinery was viewed with suspicion and, as a result, most of the work was done by hand. Finally, poor country roads kept the farmers isolated from each other and delayed the development of a wide internal market for their produce.²

Preparations for the more general practice of scientific principles were gradually made between 1837 and 1846. The Royal Agricultural Society was founded in 1840 with Queen Victoria as its patron.³ It brought the general run of farmers into contact with the methods practised by the few progressives by stimulating competition and spreading information through its publications. The rapid growth of manufacturing and commerce opened up larger markets for food products; the development of quicker and better means of trans-

---

[1] Porter, G. R., *Progress of the Nation*, Vol. I, pp. 162–3.
[2] Taken from Lord Ernle, *English Farming Past and Present*, Chapter XVII, *esp.* pp. 355–9.
[3] See Curtler, W. H. R., *A Short History of English Agriculture*, pp. 275 ff.

portation aided in this same process; joint-stock banks made credit more stable and less expensive; a new drainage system was devised; and a good deal of scientific research was done in farm problems.[1]

Most of the gain that was made in improving general farming practices between 1837 and 1846, however, was lost in the six or seven following years. For about the same time that the Royal Agricultural Society was being organised, another society was formed which aimed to arouse the country against the Corn Laws.[2] It was called the Anti-Corn Law League, and the leaders were Richard Cobden and John Bright.

In 1846, a combination of circumstances practically forced Parliament to adopt a free-trade policy toward foreign grain, much to the satisfaction of the League. Peel, the Prime Minister, introduced and secured the passage of a bill which immediately lowered the duty on wheat to 10s. a quarter when the price was under 48s. The duties on other grain were lowered in proportion and, most important of all, it was provided that on February 1, 1849, these duties were to cease. Thereafter only a nominal duty of 1s. a quarter was to be retained and this was finally abolished in 1860.[3] This Act also provided that all the duties on imports of live stock were to cease at once.

The immediate effect of these alterations in the protective system seemed to justify all that the

[1] Lord Ernle, *English Farming Past and Present*, p. 358.
[2] *Ibid.*, pp. 279 ff.
[3] Taken from Curtler, W. H. R., *op. cit.*, p. 280.

landed classes had predicted. Wheat fell from 54s. 8d. the quarter in 1846 to 38s. 6d. in 1851. The prices of other grain also declined, with the result that many farms were given up. The distress was widespread among the arable farmers but, on the other hand, stock farmers did well during this period.[1]

After 1852, the general price level began to rise accompanied by a rise in the prices of grain and meat.[2] The farmers recovered from their free trade scare and began to make improvements rapidly. The Crimean War closed the Baltic ports for a time, eliminating the competition of Russian grain and, in the next decade, the American Civil War crippled another competitor.[3] From 1853 to 1875 English farming profited from rising prices and higher land values; in fact, the period is known as "the golden age of English Agriculture."[4]

We have now surveyed the prolonged agricultural depression following the Napoleonic Wars. It is the purpose of the concluding chapter to summarise, if possible, the causes of the depression and the reasons which explain its long duration. With our results in summary form, it should be somewhat easier to estimate the effects of those relief measures actually employed and to suggest the probable results had certain other proposals and suggestions been followed.

---

[1] Curtler, *op. cit.*, p. 281.
[2] Based on Jevons' indices. See Jevons, W. S., *Investigations in Currency and Finance*, p. 150 (2).
[3] Curtler, W. H. R., *op. cit.*, p. 287.
[4] Lord Ernle, *English Farming Past and Present*, p. 370.

CHAPTER VI

SUMMARY AND CONCLUSION

An attempt has been made in the preceding pages to cover the salient economic developments in the condition of English agriculture during, approximately, the first half of the nineteenth century. The period might be divided, roughly, into two phases, namely : (1) the period of prosperity during the Wars with Napoleon and the United States ; and (2) the period of depression which began before the Wars were barely over and lasted with varying intensity until about 1852. It is the purpose of the present chapter to summarise and analyse the data bearing on these two periods. More specifically, an attempt will be made to give an answer to the following questions : (1) What were the major factors responsible for the prosperous condition of agriculture during the Wars ? (2) What were the major causes of the agricultural depression following the Wars and why was the recovery so long delayed ? (3) How effective were the farm relief measures enacted by Parliament ? (4) Could recovery have been hastened by the adoption of certain remedial measures by the farmers themselves ? and (5) What were the factors responsible for the return of another period of prosperity? The discussion will begin with the first of these questions and the others will be taken up in order.

1. AGRICULTURE DURING THE WARS

The struggle between France and England, in which Napoleon played an important part, began in 1793 and continued, with only a short interruption following the Peace of Amiens in 1802, until the Battle of Waterloo in 1815. These twenty-two years of almost continual fighting proved to be a severe economic strain on all the countries involved. The necessity of equipping an army and a navy of her own, besides furnishing funds to support those of her Allies, severely taxed England's financial resources. This burden was further increased by the two years of warfare with the United States which ended in 1814. One of the important economic effects of these Wars on England can easily be seen by tracing the trend of general wholesale prices in this period. The indices of Jevons and Silberling show that, before the Wars were over, wholesale prices had nearly doubled as compared with 1790.[1] This rapid rise is, it would seem, only to be explained by unusual and powerful economic forces operating on the demand for and the supply of goods. Since the prices of agricultural products moved in the same direction and gained as much or more over the pre-war level as did general wholesale prices, it will be worth while, in our search for an explanation of the

[1] See the chart, Chapter I, p. 29.

factors responsible for the prosperous condition of the farmers during this period, to summarise briefly the forces bearing on the supply of and the demand for goods in general. This will be done by considering, in the first place, the factors bearing on the supply of both domestic and foreign products.

The Napoleonic Wars are noted for the many and sweeping decrees issued by both combatants. Whatever may have been the ultimate purpose, the language of these orders, promulgated by Napoleon and the English Parliament, strictly forbade the subjects of the respective countries involved to engage in trade with those of the enemy country. These embargoes and blockades were only enforced with any great degree of effectiveness during a few years of their existence and, for the most part, justified the characterisation of " paper blockades." The English Government, in spite of its strict prohibition of all trade with France and her colonies, deliberately sponsored a system of licensed shipping at the outset of the Wars. Later, when the domestic crops failed to an unusual extent, the Government encouraged imports of grain from any source by means of large import bounties. In 1809 and 1810, Napoleon and the English Government decided to temporarily suspend their decrees while the French peasants disposed of their surplus grain in English markets.

Although these decrees were not successful in stopping all trade between England and the Continent, they, and the other risks connected with the war-time shipping, raised the prices of foreign

FARM RELIEF IN ENGLAND, 1813–1852

goods to English importers. Merchants seeking to trade in any French port were compelled, first of all, to secure a licence from an officer of the Crown. The price of these licences varied according to the needs of the country for imports. But, even with a licence, the uncertainties of transportation between England and the Continent were responsible for a great increase in freight and insurance rates. A comparison of these charges in 1809–12 with those prevailing in 1837 shows that the cost of shipping wheat, timber, hemp and other products was ten to fifteen times higher during the war period.[1]

Some further light on the importance of the Wars as an obstruction to the supplies of foreign goods which England usually obtained at that time is to be found by examining the indices of Professor Silberling.[2] They show that the prices of imported goods of relatively high freightage in proportion to value increased more rapidly during the early years of the period than did those of domestic production, or those with relatively low freightage in proportion to value. But it is significant to note that the prices of domestic products caught up with the prices of the goods with higher freight charges and eventually passed them.

One other set of factors bearing on the prices of imported goods during the war period which did not owe its existence to the Wars themselves

---

[1] See Chapter I, p. 25.
[2] " British Prices and Business Cycles," *Review of Economic Statistics-Supplement*, Vol. V, p. 232.

should, perhaps, be mentioned briefly. This was the protective system which had long flourished in England. It is difficult to see how this system was of any great consequence to the manufacturers during the Wars for two reasons. In the first place, English manufacturers were capable of competing profitably with foreign producers in their own home markets. Secondly, the rapid rise in English domestic prices tended to render the old protective scale of duties and import prices ineffective. The Corn Laws, intended to offer protection under ordinary conditions, were also ineffective during a large part of the war period because of the increase in domestic prices.

Thus far only those supply factors helping to explain the rise in prices during the period have been considered. There were at least two general forces which tended to lower prices by increasing the supply of goods and lowering costs of production. These were the Industrial Revolution and the Agricultural Revolution. But the effects of these forces was clearly overcome by those working in the opposite direction, some of which have been considered in the preceding discussion. A consideration of the factors bearing on the demand for goods in general will disclose still other forces making for rising prices.

Of these demand factors probably the most important was the inflation of the currency. This development was the result, as has been shown, of the financial policy of the Government which made it necessary for the Bank of England to suspend specie payments in 1797. This restriction, which later permitted the country to leave the gold standard, was originally intended as a temporary measure. Succeeding Ministries secured the continuance of the Restriction Act and, as a result, the currency was not brought back to a par with gold until 1821. As early as 1801, gold began to sell at a premium and by 1814 its price, in terms of currency, was £5 4s. per ounce—a depreciation of about 33 per cent., when measured by the old established mint price of £3 17s. 10½d. per ounce.

During this period when the currency of the Bank of England was depreciated, the number of country banks with power to issue notes increased about 400 per cent. The face value of their notes issued about tripled in the war period.[1] There was no legal restriction on the power of these country banks to extend their issues of notes and credit but it seems likely that some check on the volume of such currency and credit was provided by the Bank of England.[2] That the Bank made little effort to prevent inflation is evidenced by the fact that the circulation of its own notes increased about 300 per cent. between 1793 and 1815. The great extension of currency and credit resulting from these developments may not have been an entirely causal force raising prices, but that they could have doubled without a considerable extension of currency and credit seems improbable.

The increase in the available amount of purchasing

[1] See Chapter I, p. 28.
[2] See the argument presented in Chapter IV, p. 95.

power was not the only demand factor tending to raise prices. The population of England and Wales, which had increased but slowly between 1700 and 1760, began to grow rapidly after 1760 and continued to increase at the rate of 1½ per cent. per year during the war period. There was also an increased demand for munitions and other goods necessary to equip the army and navy of the country. The expenditures of the Government for such goods amounted to about £50,000 annually.

The important forces accounting for the rapid rise in the general price level during the Wars can thus be summed up as follows : (1) an increase in the cost of foreign goods and raw materials due to the obstructions to trade during the Wars ; and (2) an increased domestic demand for goods due to a larger volume of currency and credit, a growing population, and Government purchases for carrying on the struggle against France.

It has already been pointed out that agricultural prices rose about as much as did general wholesale prices, and it seems probable that all of the factors mentioned in connection with the analysis of the movement of general prices had a good deal to do with the trend which farm prices took. There are, however, several factors peculiar to agricultural prices which should be mentioned. In the first place, it should be noted that, although the general effect of the Agricultural Revolution was to increase production, the domestic supplies of grain were, on the whole, considered insufficient to supply the home market at ordinary prices during the war period. Out of the twenty-two years of war the harvests of only two were abundant, fourteen were decidedly deficient, and seven of these were poor enough to arouse fears of a famine. The prices of grain, at least, might not have risen to such heights as they did in 1796–7, 1800–2 and 1812 had it not been that the foreign supply of grain, on which the country usually depended, was seriously interfered with by war activities. The result of the widely variable seasons is clearly shown by the chart of grain prices in Chapter I, p. 31. Meat prices show the same trend as those of grain but moved upward without such wide fluctuations.

It has been pointed out that the population was increasing rapidly during this period of poor seasons. Along with this increase in numbers there was a movement away from villages, and a growth of towns and cities as the Industrial Revolution changed the methods of producing goods. This development was of considerable importance for the farmers, as it tended to make the population less self-sufficient and thus opened up new markets for dairy produce, meat and vegetables.

The combined effect of all these various factors was sufficient, as we have seen, to double the wholesale prices of farm products between 1793 and 1815. The landlords, tenants and independent farm owners responded to these higher prices by adopting higher standards of living, improving and extending the acreage under cultivation, and by introducing, in some cases, greatly improved methods of cultivation and cattle raising. Land values increased rapidly and rents rose, in general, about 50 per cent. Practically everyone, of course, considered the high prices to be permanent.

For a time, the expenses of the farmers seemed to lag behind the rising prices of their products but soon increasing costs began to narrow profit margins. The wages of agricultural labourers did not increase as rapidly as did the wholesale prices of farm products, but they eventually rose higher and showed little tendency to fall along with agricultural prices.[1] National taxes were increased to cover the heavy expense of carrying on a long war and the Poor Rates increased about 400 per cent. over the pre-war payments. The table given in Chapter I, p. 35, shows that the farmer's other expenses of production had about doubled by the end of the Wars. But as long as prices continued to rise there was little complaint from the agriculturalists. Under conditions of falling prices these expenses, some of which did not respond to changes in the price level, seemed a tremendous burden.

2. THE FIRST YEARS OF DEPRESSION

Toward the latter part of 1813 a striking reversal in the trend of grain prices became manifest. It will be recalled that, in 1812, grain had sold at famine prices, the wholesale price of wheat, for example, being 155s. at one time. But the grain market did not maintain these prices for long and

[1] Taken from Bowley, A. L., "Agricultural Wages," *Journal of the Royal Statistical Society*, Vol. 61, pp. 702–22.

in September 1813 there began a decline which continued into the first few months of 1816. In the course of about two years, the average price of corn (all grain) declined nearly 50 per cent. as compared with the 1812 average, and over 40 per cent. as compared with the 1813 average.[1] The grain growers became panic-stricken and, as we have seen, brought strong pressure to bear on Parliament for some sort of relief.

The case of the mixed farmers, and those who confined their attention almost entirely to the production of meat, wool and dairy products, was somewhat different from that of the large grain raisers of the eastern section of England. Meat, cheese and wool maintained their war-time prices up to about the end of 1814.[2] When the prices of these products dropped from 20 to 30 per cent. between 1814 and 1817, the grass farmers joined with the grain growers in protesting against the heavy Poor-Rates, Tithes and the inactivity of Parliament.

It was this series of events which precipitated a period of economic depression in English agriculture which caused many to fail. In the case of those farmers on strong clay lands who managed to hang on, there was little improvement until after 1835, and farming in general did not experience another era of real prosperity until after 1850. Not every year in the period between 1813 and 1837 was one

---

[1] Taken from Jevons' indices, *Investigations in Currency and Finance*, pp. 144–5.
[2] *Ibid.*, pp. 144–5.

of adversity for the grain growers, and other classes of farmers fared even better; there were short periods of rising prices which brought some relief. It was such an event that mitigated some of the distress occasioned by the precipitous decline of prices between 1813 and 1816; the rise in prices between the fall of 1816 and 1819 actually convinced some farmers that their troubles would soon be over. Since this first period of distress is to be explained in part, at least, by the operation of certain economic forces which were not operative throughout the whole of the depression, it will be worth while to pause here for a brief analysis of the causal factors involved. This discussion will centre about the movements of agricultural prices and will begin with an analysis of the supply factors.

From the point of view of some writers,[1] the supply factors were by far the most important force in bringing about this great fall in the prices of farm products. They argue that the relaxation of restraints on trade and the consequent decline in the cost of production of goods, brought about by the defeat of Napoleon and the establishment of peace with the United States, constitute one important change making for lower prices in general, particularly in the case of grain. It is pointed out that Napoleon's power began to wane after his disastrous Russian campaign in the winter of 1812, and from then on until his exile to Elba in the summer of 1814 there was a constant relaxation of the barriers to trade with England. As

[1] See Tooke, T., *History of Prices*.

Napoleon's system weakened, the English also relaxed their restrictions on trade. The result was that by 1815 the foreign trade of the country had begun to resume its peace-time character and raw materials, grain and other products were to be had much more cheaply in England. This relaxation in trade barriers made it possible, it is pointed out, for a considerable quantity (about 1,600,000 quarters of wheat and oats) of foreign grain to enter the country in 1814. Furthermore, the mere prospect of peace had sufficient psychological effect to bring a fall in prices as early as 1813.

The argument emphasising the importance of supply factors is, perhaps, even more strongly supported by an analysis of the crops of 1813 and 1815. It is well to keep in mind that the four harvests preceding that of 1813 were all considerably below the average. The resulting high prices probably encouraged the expansion of acreage and the introduction of improvements, but to what extent it is impossible to tell. At any rate, the weather during the spring and summer of 1813 was unusually favourable and the result was a bumper harvest of all grains. The price of wheat began to decline in September, and by December it had fallen almost 40 per cent. The prices of oats, barley, peas, beans and rye behaved in a similar manner. It would seem, then, that this unusually large harvest was one of the most important, if not the prime factor, in precipitating the decline in grain prices.

The harvest of 1814 did not turn out as well as

that of the previous year but the large carry-over from 1813, coupled with the importation of 1,600,000 quarters of foreign oats and wheat, more than checked any tendency for prices to rise. Then came another bumper crop in 1815 and prices moved still lower. But, admitting the importance of these supply factors, it does not seem probable that they afford a full explanation of the trend of grain prices, much less those of meat, wool and cheese, after 1814. Some part of the continued fall of prices is to be explained by a decline in the domestic demand for agricultural produce.

One of the factors responsible for a decline in demand for farm products was the industrial and commercial depression into which the country was plunged in the early part of 1815. It is not necessary here to go into all of the details regarding the effect of this depression but it is significant to note that the wholesale prices of all commodities, according to the indices of Jevons and Silberling, show a 20 per cent. drop between 1814 and 1816. Prices on the Continent and in the United States also fell at the same time. Falling prices, both at home and abroad, caused English manufacturers to curtail production and lay off men. At the same time, the supply of labour was considerably increased by the discharge of about 300,000 soldiers and sailors. Ex-soldiers without money or a job, and wage-earners without work were poor customers for farm products. And, when the Government cut down the size of the land and naval forces, it also curtailed its purchases of food products. It was unfortunate for the farmers that the demand for their products should fall off just when the supplies, particularly in the case of grain, happened to be the largest in some time.

This fall of farm prices, and of wholesale prices in general, is also related to another factor—a financial force—which also tended to lower prices by decreasing the demand for goods. Between 1813 and 1816, 92 country banks failed and a total of 240 suspended cash payments. In some country districts there was a great contraction of the country bank notes following such failures and, although there is no accurate information on the matter, it seems probable that the banks were forced to restrict loans as well.

The contraction of currency and credit due to the failure of these banks tended to lower prices in the locality of each particular bank. Since the circulation of the notes of any one bank was quite limited, the failure of one might not be expected to have a great effect on the general price level of the whole country. But the absolute failure of 92 of these banks, plus the suspension of payments by many more, would tend to lower prices in a number of districts. Farmers, or dealers, in one such district seeking to take advantage of higher prices in the vicinity of the Bank of England would find many others doing the same thing, and the pressure of additional stocks of goods might force prices down there. It is quite unnecessary, of course, to point out that these surmises in no way prove that the failure of the country banks had precisely these effects on farm prices.[1] But it seems quite probable that such large reductions in the amount of purchasing power had an adverse effect on farmers' incomes.

Faced with ruin if prices continued to fall, the farmers, particularly the landlords, made use of their great political strength to enlist the aid of Parliament. After taking up the major part of nearly two Parliamentary sessions with debates on the merits of protection for the English grain growers, they finally secured the passage of a new Corn Law in 1815. This measure raised the prices at which wheat could be imported from 63s. to 80s. the quarter. When the average domestic price was below 80s., no wheat could come in at all. Farmers were generally agreed that 80s. would be a remunerative price and the advocates of the new law hoped that it would keep the price of wheat at about this level. The prices governing the imports of other grain were raised in the same proportion as that of wheat.

The new Corn Law was a disappointment to many farmers because prices did not rise immediately. But it probably did aid them by keep-

---

[1] Whether the failure of the country banks was a cause or a result of the fall of farm prices is a question not easily settled. Probably it was both cause and effect. There seems to be some reason, however, to suppose that it was the failure of the debtors of these banks, namely, the farmers, who were responsible for putting the banks into dangerous positions. If this was the case, the fall in prices, assuming that to be the cause of the failure of the farmers, must have been well begun before there was any appreciable reduction in the currency and credit of the country banks. The reduction of purchasing power must have been a contributory rather than a precipitating cause.

ing out foreign grain at a time when the home markets were over-stocked. Temporary relief seemed to come from non-legislative sources. The general wholesale price level rose somewhat between 1816 and 1819 and the prices of farm products regained some of the ground lost in the period 1813-16. This partial recovery created the impression among some farmers that their troubles were over, but they soon discovered their mistake.

3. Depression and Recovery, 1819-52

The upward trend of grain prices came to an end in the latter part of 1818. Between that year and 1823, the average price of corn (all grain) fell off 54 per cent.—an even greater decline than occurred between 1812 and 1816.[1] These relatively low prices continued, with the exception of some few years, until after 1852. In 1850 the average price of grain was 57 per cent. below the highest war-time yearly average and 36 per cent. below the average for 1782. This great decline more than offset the gain in prices made during the Wars and points to one of the major causes of the agricultural depression.

The grain growers, however, were not the only class of farmers who suffered from falling prices.

[1] The per cent. decline in the prices of both grain and meat was greater than the fall in the general price level between 1818 and 1823. A comparison of the relative prices of agricultural commodities with those comprising Jevons' all commodity index, using the averages for 1782 as a base for both, shows that, even though the percentage decline in this period was greater, grain and meat prices had not fallen as much as had non-agricultural commodities.

After 1820 the dairy farmers and cattle raisers found themselves in much the same situation as were the arable farmers. The wholesale prices of meats (beef and mutton) fell about 34 per cent. between 1820 and 1823—a change almost as great as in the case of grain. The trend of meat prices continued downward, with some few exceptions, until after 1846 and, at the lowest point, the yearly average was approximately 50 per cent. below the peak of war-time prices.

But the farmers were not the only ones faced with the problem of getting a living under conditions of falling prices. The indices of general wholesale prices show a sharp drop of about 30 per cent. in the general price level between 1818 and 1823. As in the case of agricultural products, the trend continued downward until about 1850. In 1849 the average for all commodities was about 60 per cent. below the highest average for any year during the Wars and 36 per cent. below the average for 1782. That is to say, general wholesale prices, in the thirty-five years following the Wars, not only lost all the ground gained during the twenty-two years of rising prices but fell considerably below the pre-war level.[1]

This coincidence in the movement of agricultural prices and those of commodities in general was of considerable significance for the farmers. It meant that, at the very time when an increase in demand would have helped to mitigate the severe effects

[1] All of these data on prices are taken from Jevons' indices found in *Investigations in Currency and Finance*, pp. 144-5.

FARM RELIEF IN ENGLAND, 1813-1852

of two or three large crops, the ability of the manufacturing population to buy goods was seriously curtailed by an industrial and commercial depression. The manufacturing industries began to recover as early as the fall of 1821 when the farmers were still experiencing the ruinous effects of low prices. The delayed recovery of agriculture becomes more difficult to explain when one considers that the trend of both non-agricultural and agricultural prices was the same throughout the period 1818 to 1850. The grain raisers, as has been pointed out, found their situation little improved before 1837 and, although those farmers who practised diversified farming and cattle raising were somewhat better off, agriculture as a whole did not experience a period of real prosperity until after 1852.

The following analysis of this long period of depression attempts to give some answer to each of the following questions:

(1) What were the major causes of the depression?

(2) Why did agriculture fail to recover as rapidly as did the manufacturing and commercial industries?

(3) Did the arable farmers suffer more than the grass farmers?

(4) Did the wealthy landlords bear the brunt of falling prices or did farmers both large and small suffer equally?

(5) What was done by the farmers and the Government to mitigate the effects of falling prices?

Would the adoption of certain programmes have greatly helped the farmers?

(6) How did the condition of agriculture at the end of the depression period compare with its status in the war and pre-war periods?

(7) What were the major factors responsible for the return of prosperity after 1850?

One of the major causes of the depression was, of course, the great fall in the prices of farm products. The effects of this sudden reversal of price movements do not need to be discussed in great detail here. It is sufficient to note that the incomes of farmers, and the value of their lands, buildings, equipment, and livestock were all lowered in proportion to the fall in prices. What we would like to know is why the prices of farm products dropped when they did and why they continued to move downward as long as they did. Since general wholesale prices show the same marked decline after 1818 and continued to fall just about as long as did agricultural prices, some analysis of the more general forces bearing on all prices in the period may be helpful.

When one attempts to find the cause of the downward trend of prices in England following 1818, the striking resemblance between the behaviour of wholesale prices in the United States and those in England cannot escape notice. Not only was there a similar decline in both countries after 1814, but in both countries the recovery came at about the same time, namely, 1852. These facts suggest that, if one is to find all of the causal factors involved in the English situation, the inquiry would have to take into consideration forces of an international character.[1] Such an investigation would be considerably outside the scope of this study.

There is a possibility, however, that some part of the similarity of price movements in the two countries, particularly in the ten years following 1815, can be explained as the result of similar financial policies of the respective Governments. In the United States the method of financing the War of 1812, coupled with a poorly regulated banking system, led to inflation and it took six or seven years to put credit and currency on a sound gold standard basis. We have seen that England abandoned the gold standard during the Wars and that the Government was pledged to repeal the Bank Restriction Act six months after peace with Napoleon should be established. But six months after Waterloo, the Ministry considered it unwise to compel the Bank to pay gold for its notes and the Restriction was extended to 1819.

Before the actual date for resumption of specie payments set by law arrived, both Houses of Parliament appointed Select Committees to investigate the condition of the Bank and to advise their respective Houses as to the proper legislation relative to actual resumption. The House of

---

[1] Some of these forces would be: the world production of gold, the use of credit instruments; the velocity of circulation of money and credit; the volume of world trade; costs of production, and transportation of goods; the factors bearing on the supply of goods in general; and, probably, still others.

Commons Committee, headed by Robert Peel, made a careful study of the situation and the major recommendations of this Committee were passed by both Houses. The statute, known as Peel's Bill, provided for a return to specie payments by the Bank within a period of four years. In order to protect the gold reserve of the Bank, it was provided that only large amounts of notes could be converted at a ratio not far from the market value of gold, during the first few months following the adoption of the Bill. The actual return to the gold standard was accomplished by 1821, when there no longer existed any difference between the market and mint prices of gold.

One result of the adoption of Peel's Bill is to be seen by a subsequent examination of the circulation of the Bank of England, and the value of country bank notes stamped. On August 31, 1819, the circulation of the Bank of England stood at £25,252,690, and on August 31, 1822, it was down to £17,464,790, a decline of about 30 per cent. Between 1818 and 1823, the face value of country bank notes stamped fell 43 per cent., a development which seems to lend support to the argument that the circulation of the Bank of England tended to determine that of the country banks.

Just how important this financial factor was to the farmers it would be difficult to say. It certainly was not the only cause of the fall in the prices of grain, at least, in the period 1819 to 1823. One must consider the effects of the business depression on the demand for food products and also the fact that in three successive years, namely, 1820, 1821 and 1822, the harvests were unusually abundant.

Although these supply factors were probably of considerable importance in the case of grain, it is difficult to see how they could have been responsible to any great extent for the fall in meat, wool and cheese prices. Large supplies of grain resulting from three favourable harvests do not explain the plight of the grass farmers. Even in the case of grains, it is doubtful if there existed a condition of "over-production" between 1818 and 1823, and it is much more doubtful if this was the case after 1823. Support for this statement can be found by examining the indices of Professor Jevons.

In the year when the prices of grain were lowest, namely, 1822, Jevons' index number of general wholesale prices stands at 88 and his index for the average prices of all grains is 92. Taking the index number of wholesale prices as a base, it appears that, relative to 1782, the prices of grain were about 5 per cent. above those of the forty commodities, including grain, which made up his all-commodity index. The same general relationship between these two classes of prices was maintained throughout the entire period of the agricultural depression. Indeed, for the most part, grain prices were from 50 to 70 per cent. above those of the averages of all commodities, and approximately the same thing was true in the case of meat.

The farmers loudly complained of the disastrous effects of foreign competition in the period 1818 to 1823 and urged that Parliament again raise the prices at which grain could be imported. It is difficult to find any substantial factual basis for such a diagnosis of the distress, since only a small quantity of oats, about 700,000 quarters, entered the country from foreign countries during the period. The Corn Law gave the home growers practically a monopoly of the domestic market. No more than that could be accomplished by a further upward revision of prices and duties.

The producers of meat were even better protected under the law than the grain growers. Importations of live stock were absolutely forbidden and the lack of cold storage facilities made it virtually impossible for foreign cattle raisers to compete strongly in the fresh-meat market. The legal restrictions on imports of foreign livestock were practically abolished in 1846, along with the repeal of the Corn Laws, and then both the grass and arable farmers felt the full effects of foreign competition. But it does not seem possible to attribute to this factor any great responsibility for the agricultural depression, even in the case of the grain growers, until these restrictive laws were rescinded.

So far only the factors bearing on the incomes of farmers have been discussed. It will be worth while to examine their various expense items to see if the outlay for these decreased along with the falling prices of farm products. If the farmer's expenses failed to fall in proportion to his change in income, then that would seem to be a big factor in explaining the distress.

There are, unfortunately, no indices of the cost of living for farmers' families in this period. There is not even a reliable series of retail prices of the goods farmers bought. This lack of data makes it impossible to measure the purchasing power of their incomes with any great degree of accuracy. It is possible, however, to make a rough approximation based on the indices of general wholesale prices and the indices of wholesale prices of farm products. As has been pointed out, grain and meat prices were, relative to 1782, from 40 to 50 per cent. above general wholesale prices. If these prices of grain fairly represent those received by farmers, and, if the retail prices of goods farmers bought remained within this range of 40 to 50 per cent., there seems to be no reason for attributing any great part of the depression to a discrepancy between incomes and expenditures.

There were outlays, other than those for goods, about which we do have more precise information. These include the Poor-Rates, tithes, and the National taxes. There was little, if any, decline in the assessments for the Poor Fund before the Poor-Law revision of 1834 and these payments were a heavy burden on the agriculturists, heavier in fact, than on any other class. And, although there were reductions from time to time, the National taxes were also a heavy burden. Before the depression was over they had been reduced about 50 per cent. but it should be remembered that the purchasing power of money about doubled at the same time. In addition to these more or less fixed expenses, there were tithe payments which farmers had to make. In some cases these had been changed from payments in goods to a definite money payment and those who had made such arrangements found the rates increasingly burdensome under conditions of falling prices. It was not until about 1836 that this situation was remedied by a commutation of all tithes into fixed money payments which varied, from then on, according to the purchasing power of money.

Most of the work on the farms at that time was done by hand, since there was relatively little machinery available compared to modern conditions, and relatively few farmers would use what labour-saving devices had been invented. Consequently, the wages which farmers paid in relation to the prices of farm products is a factor worthy of some consideration. Bowley's indices of the wages of English agricultural labour show that money wages rose slowly during the war period but continued to move upward until 1833. Then they slowly receded until, in 1850, they were back to the 1824 level. It seems, therefore, that wages rose at a time when nearly all other prices were falling. Farmers, under the circumstances, would have done well to have economised on wage outlays as much as possible.

The factors responsible for the agricultural depression which have been discussed thus far can be summarised briefly as follows : (1) falling prices of farm products brought about in part, at least, by (*a*) the Bank of England's return to specie payments; (b) the severe industrial and commercial depression, resulting in a decrease in demand for farm products between 1819 and 1821; (c) the unusually abundant harvests of 1820, 1821 and 1822; (2) the failure of expenses such as wages, tithes, poor rates, and national taxes to come down in proportion to the fall in the prices of farm products.

Perhaps the question as to why agriculture did not recover as rapidly as did other industries can be answered, in part at least, by pointing out certain differences in the characters of farmers and business men, and also some of the differences between farming and manufacturing in England at that time.

Some of the differences between the English farmers and the business men in the first half of the nineteenth century, which are still true in the twentieth century, were: (1) The farmers were as a whole less enterprising and more tied down by customs than were business men; (2) For many farmers, farming was mainly a way of living rather than a means of making profits. Consequently, they paid less attention to costs of production and the possibilities of developing new markets than did business men; (3) Even if farming was not satisfactory most farmers hesitated to give it up because of (a) established family ties and traditions; (b) the uncertainties of finding a job for which they were adapted; (c) the sacrifice which they would have to make in selling out at prevailing prices; and (d) the possibility that brighter times were ahead. A considerable number were forced to give up their farms but many continued, just barely holding on.

Certain inherent differences between farming and manufacturing help to explain the relatively tardy recovery in the former industry. In the first place, farmers were more dependent on the weather and their assets were more susceptible to destruction by disease than was the case in manufacturing industries. Secondly, manufacturers had more opportunities to lower their costs by adopting large-scale methods of production and labour-saving devices than did the farmers. This was a big advantage to manufacturers in this period of falling prices. Thirdly, the more rapid turnover of capital in manufacturing was an advantage under conditions of falling prices. And in the fourth place, English manufacturers were capturing more and more of the world markets for their products in the period before 1850. English farmers could not meet foreign competition and, therefore, had to rely on the domestic market. These differences, however, were probably not sufficient to account entirely for the relative positions of agriculture and manufacturing during the period. An examination of the available data on the condition of agriculture at the end of the depression seems to indicate that some classes of farmers fared better than others. Perhaps some part of the farmer's difficulties was due to the failure to make the most out of an expanding internal market.

A good deal of support for such a conclusion is

afforded by the observations made by James Caird in his survey of the agricultural situation in 1850–1.[1] It will be recalled that it was the grain growers who complained the most during the depression. Caird suggests that the explanation of this is to be found in the fact that the price of meat did not fall to the same extent as did that of grain. A comparison of Jevons' indices of these two classes of prices does not support this statement. There seems to have been no appreciable discrepancy between the relative prices of these products during most of the depression. It is true, however, that meat prices were relatively higher in the years when he made his tour.

When Caird compared his findings with the situation in 1770, the year in which Young made his tours, he found that the grass and mixed types of farming had become more profitable than grain growing. This conclusion he supported with the following observations. The average size of the domestic wheat crop was about 14 per cent. larger in 1850 than in 1770, but the price of bread was practically the same. The prices of meat had risen 70 per cent., wool over 100 per cent., and butter 100 per cent. in the same period. Rents on arable land had doubled, but in 1850 the rents in the grain-growing counties of the east coast averaged 23s. 8d. the acre, while the average on the grass and mixed farms of the midlands and west was 31s. 5d. This difference, he thought, could be explained by the

[1] See his *English Agriculture in* 1850–1851, especially the concluding chapters.

growth of population, the movement toward the towns and cities, and the increase in the wages of manufacturing and agricultural labourers. There had been, therefore, a greater increase in demand for meat, vegetables and dairy produce than for grain products.

If these facts accurately describe the relative positions of the various classes of farmers, it is easier to understand why it was the representatives from the grain-growing districts who made the greatest demands on Parliament for relief. In many cases the landlords spoke for themselves and it is fair to presume, from the lack of petitions from their tenants, that the brunt of the depression rested largely on the landlord's pocket-book. Tenants also suffered for a time because of heavy taxes and the loss of a large part of their investments in their farms, but the prevalence of short term leases enabled them to shift the burden to the landlord.

The next question is what, if anything, could be done under the circumstances to mitigate the effects of the sudden reversal of prices on the tenants and landlords of the grain-growing sections. We can begin by seeing how Parliament treated them.

4. Farm Relief Programmes

With the growth of manufacturing and commerce in England during the first half of the nineteenth century, the political influence of the landed class began to wane. At the time when the farmers

FARM RELIEF IN ENGLAND, 1813-1852 169

first began to feel the injurious effects of falling prices (1813), Parliament was still pretty much under the control of the agricultural classes and the Corn Law of 1815 was the result. Subsequent Ministries proved to be less amenable to the desires of the agriculturists, but they were quite free with " Select Committees to Investigate the Distressed State of Agriculture." Such committees sat in 1821, 1822, 1833 and 1835-6. The reports which they presented to Parliament were, on the whole, valuable sources of information but English farmers were inclined to regard all of them as failures because in no case did they result, directly, in relief legislation. It is possible that these reports influenced the Government to pass such indirect measures as the Tithe Commutation Act and the Poor-Law Revision Act but they certainly resulted in no legislative measure to raise the prices paid to the farmers for meat and grain.

The Select Committee, which reported to the House of Commons in 1821, found the conditions of the agriculturists to be just about as bad as the farmers petitioning for relief had said they were. But, after examining all the witnesses and collecting a great deal of data, it came to the conclusion that the farmers' problems could not be solved by legislation. Interference with the operation of economic forces, it said, might easily do more harm than good. It, therefore, would recommend to the House none of the relief plans suggested. The farmers would have to work out their own salvation.

Although it was recognised at the time that this

Committee did not include a fair number of representatives of agriculture, its able survey of the situation of the farmers and the opinions which it expressed carried great weight with Parliament. The farmers likened the report to a treatise on Political Economy, that dismal science, but the manufacturing and commercial classes found their own views well and forcefully stated by influential men.

Whether the Committee was right or wrong in maintaining that the legislature could do nothing for the farmer cannot be ascertained, since even the remedies suggested were not tried. Parliament, however, did give the farmers higher protection in 1815 when they asked for it and kept them sheltered from the full force of foreign competition until 1846. Later, two other measures, namely the Poor-Law Revision Act of 1834 and the Tithe Commutation Act of 1836, were passed with the intention of relieving some of the farmers' burdens. A brief examination of the effects of these measures, together with an analysis of the possible results had some of the most important proposed remedies been adapted, may throw some light on the soundness of the Committee's position. We shall begin with the Corn Laws.

The farmers hoped that the effect of the Corn Law of 1815 would be to keep the average prices of grain about equal to those at which foreign grain could be imported. In other words, they thought the law would practically set minimum, but not maximum, prices. The prices per quarter set by law above which foreign grain could be admitted were as follows : wheat, 80s. ; rye, peas and beans, 53s. ; barley, beer or bigg, 40s. ; oats, 26s. When the average home price was lower than that set by law, no foreign grain could come in but above these prices imports were admitted free.

That the law failed to accomplish all the farmers expected is obvious. Wheat sold at an average of 63s. in 1815, 43s. in 1822 and, with the exception of the years 1817 and 1818, it remained below this relatively high price of 80s. throughout the period of the depression. The prices of other grains behaved in a similar manner. But, even though the law was not entirely successful from the farmer's point of view, it did, undoubtedly, prevent the prices of grain from falling as far as they otherwise might have during the period of the depression. This was especially true in the years 1815, 1820, 1821, and 1822 when the distress of the farmers was probably the most severe. Whether the farmers benefited in the long run from the shelter thus provided has been questioned.[1]

The other legislative measures which were intended to aid the farmers, namely, the Poor-Law Revision and the Tithe Commutation Act, were beneficial but of minor importance. The new system of administering the poor funds reduced the number of parish paupers and thereby reduced the local taxes which were a burden on the farmers of

[1] See Curtler, W. H. R., *A Short History of English Agriculture*, pp. 278–9. He quotes Tooke's opinion that more severe competition would have forced the English farmers to have improved their farming practices and lowered their costs of production sooner than they did.

the parish. The Tithe Commutation Act also tended to ease the expenses of the farmers by making all tithes payable in money, the amount of which was to vary with its purchasing power. The owners of tithes received fixed incomes in terms of goods and the farmers were not overly burdened in subsequent periods of falling prices. Both of these measures probably helped the agriculturists to adjust themselves to lower prices and might well have been enacted sooner.

These last two measures which have been considered were scarcely regarded as farm relief legislation by the agriculturists. They wanted something from Parliament which would measurably increase farmers' incomes without any great additional effort on their part. Most of the suggestions were made in the years of greatest distress, namely 1814–16 and 1820–3. The outstanding ideas were: (1) the restoration of remunerative prices and a more just settlement of the internal debt of the country by inflating the currency; (2) Government purchases of grain to be sold abroad; (3) Government loans to individuals who were willing to buy up grain to be stored and marketed at a later date; and (4) the restoration of the export bounty on grain.[1]

The return to an inflated state of the currency might have necessitated the abandonment of the

[1] It is interesting to note the similarity between these proposals and those which were made in the United States following the World War. The United States Government is now trying out a scheme to encourage orderly marketing very much like the third suggestion.

gold standard again. Should this have happened there would have been no check, other than that provided by the Government and the Bank of England, on the extension of currency and credit. The injurious effects which fluctuating prices would have had on the other industries of the country would have been too dear a price to pay for the relief of one single industry. It is doubtful if prices could be stabilised at their war-time level, once it was reached, unless other countries could be persuaded to co-operate. Since this was practically impossible, this suggestion seems to have been a dangerous, costly, and uncertain way of relieving a debtor class such as the farmers then were.

The remaining three proposals were advanced as measures primarily intended to relieve a temporary situation of agricultural distress arising from an overstocked condition of the markets, or "overproduction." It has been pointed out that, according to the indices of Jevons, there was little if any overproduction of grain as compared with other commodities in any of the years of the depression, even in the period 1820-3 when these measures were proposed. That the distress was not entirely ephemeral was clearly demonstrated with the passing of time. Finally, it is questionable whether a condition of overproduction such as was assumed, can be best remedied by the adoption of measures which tend to raise the price of the good, the supply of which is supposed to be too great. Would not raising the price of wheat, or keeping it from falling as far as it otherwise might by artificial means, preclude the possibility of reaching a state of readjustment when the measures might be withdrawn without a change in the status of the producers?

There would have been still further objections to putting the Government into the grain market, or to the restoration of the export bounty on grain. The cost to the Government would have been great in either case because in the period 1820–3 the prices of grain were unusually low in most other countries. Consequently, with prices higher in England than abroad, a government-owned surplus of grain could have been sold in foreign markets only at a considerable sacrifice. In the case of the export bounty plan, the difference in price between domestic and foreign grain would have been continually widened by exports from England, necessitating higher and higher bounties to make exportation profitable for the farmers. Both taxpayers and consumers would naturally have strong objections to both of these plans.

Of these temporary relief measures, that which came the closest to being adopted was the proposal that the Government encourage individuals to relieve the " overproduction " situation by loaning them money on grain purchased at current prices and stored in government warehouses. Out of a fund of £1,000,000, the Government was to advance loans up to two-thirds of the market value of the warehoused grain whenever the home price, in the case of wheat, was under 60s. Interest at the rate of 3 per cent. and warehouse charges were to be paid by the individuals, and the grain could only be withdrawn when all accounts with the Government were settled. It was expected that the farmers would derive a good deal of benefit from a more orderly marketing of grain such as the scheme would encourage.

There was a possibility that the Government, as a creditor, might be forced directly into the grain market under this plan should prices fall more than one-third after the loan was made. In such an event, the individual grain dealers would probably let the Government collect its loans by selling the grain. But it happened that the average price of wheat, the most important of the grains, averaged 44s. 7d. for the year 1822 when the plan was proposed. The lowest monthly average price at which wheat sold during this year, and for many years after 1822, was 38s. 10d., which was considerably above two-thirds of 44s. 7d. It seems probable that this proposal, if it had been enacted, would have mitigated the severity of the distress in 1822 without putting the Government directly into the grain business. Whether this programme would have become a permanent government policy toward agriculture had it proven successful, and whether permanent aid of this kind would have been desirable, it is difficult to say.

We have yet to consider the non-legislative relief measures which might have been adopted. Curtler says that the Scotch farmers who " farmed highly " weathered the storm.

"Instead of repeatedly calling on Parliament to help them [he points out] they had helped themselves, by spending large sums in draining and manuring the land; they had adopted the subsoil plough, and the drainage system of Smith of Deanston, used machinery to economise labour, and improved the breed of stock."[1]

While there were some enterprising farmers in England who kept up with the programme followed by the best of the Scotchmen, little progress in this direction had been made by most of them prior to 1835.

When Caird[2] made his study of the agricultural situation in 1850–1, he found that landlords, in general, knew little about farm problems and methods, and that their agents were equally ignorant. He urged that the landlords make a serious study of agriculture, or as an alternative, hire competent agents to represent them, suggesting that the high war-time prices had been responsible for the careless attitude which had been taken. Although it was true that bread was still the staple for the great mass of consumers, farmers should take advantage of the fact, he said, that labouring classes in general were consuming a great deal more meat and cheese than formerly. He called the attention of the owners of the large grain-growing farms of the East to the fact that the smaller, diversified farms in the Midland and Western sections of the country were paying higher rents

[1] Curtler, W. H. R., *A Short History of English Agriculture*, p. 271.
[2] Caird, Sir James, *English Agriculture in 1850–1851*, p. 492.

and were, in general, more profitable. Finally, landlords should begin to give longer leases to their tenants in order to encourage improvements which were so badly needed.

Caird's survey is probably the best description we have of the condition of agriculture at the close of the long depression. It indicates that most farmers did not make any great amount of effort to help themselves during the depression, particularly those grain growers on the heavy clay lands who suffered most. That this class of farmers could have mitigated the effects of falling prices, seems to be indicated by the results obtained on the diversified farms and those on which improvements and labour-saving devices were used.

Although the agriculturists made notable strides toward a general higher plane of farming during the ten years following 1850, this one development alone was not entirely responsible for the decided recovery of agriculture. The general level of wholesale prices increased over 28 per cent. between 1850 and 1860, and the wholesale prices of agricultural products also gained as much or more during the same period.[1] Another factor decidedly favourable to the farmers, especially the grain growers, was the difficulty of obtaining grain from foreign countries due to the Crimean Wars, and later the Civil War. Consequently, although foreign competition was no longer restricted, imports supplemented, but did not displace, the domestic production. So great

[1] Taken from Sauerbeck's indices, *Journal of the Royal Statistical Society*, Vol. 49, pp. 634 and 648.

was the general improvement among the agriculturists, and so much progress was made, that the period has been called the "Golden Age" of English agriculture.

INDEX

Agriculture, Board of. *See* Board of Agriculture

Agriculture, depression in:
and recovery (1819–52), 155;
Caird's views on, 167–8;
causes of, 158–65;
first years of, 148–55;
See also McCulloch, J. R., Porter, G. R., Tooke, T., and Ricardo, D.

Agriculture, distress of:
becomes general, 155–6;
causes of, 67–9, (1822) 117–18, (1833) 128, analysed, 148–54;
Committee on (1820), 97, (1821) 102, (1833) 128, (1836) 135;
continued (1817–19), 90–1;
crash of 1825, 125;
deepens (1820), 97;
effect on tenants and landlords, 70–9;
following 1846, 139;
opinions on (1821–2), 114–18;
overstated (1833), 129–30;

Agriculture, distress of:
reports on (1821), 102, (1833) 126; (1836) 136;
See also Board of Agr., Agr., relief of, Commons, Committees

Agriculture, general:
about 1800, 1 ff.;
condition of, 167–8;
lack of progress in, 9;
markets and transportation, 15;
necessary changes in, 10;
population, 7;
progress of, 129–32;
See also Agr., depression in, Agr., distress of, Agr., industries of, Agr., labourers in, Agr., prices, Agr., progress of, Agr., relief of, Agr., revolution in

Agriculture, industries of:
effect of low prices on, 114–16;
general state of (1793–1815), 30–6;
relative distress among (1836), 136;

Agriculture, industries of:
  relative importance of, 2–5;
  relative prosperity of, 167–8;
  unscientific practices in, 137;
  See also Agr., general, Crops
Agriculture, labourers in:
  condition of (1822), 117, (1833) 129;
  effect of Poor Law revision on, 133;
  state of (1814–16), 74;
  See also Poor Laws, Wages
Agriculture, population of:
  decrease in (1811–31), 131;
  size of (1801), 7–8;
  See also Agr., labourers in, Landlords, Population, Porter, G. R., Tenants
Agriculture, prices:
  analysis of decline in, 150–4;
  compared with non-agr., 156;
  Corn (all grains) (1780–1860), 31;
  during Wars, 46–8;
  effect of on farmers, 31–6;
  effect of Corn Law repeal on, 138–9;
  fall of (1814–16), 65;
  in (1820), 101, (1824–7) 122, (1822–5) 121, (1850–60) 177;
  meat (1780–1860), 31;

Agriculture, prices:
  movement of (1810–22), 66;
  relative movement of to 1850, 167;
  relative status of (1833), 127;
  reversal of trend in, 149;
  showing "overproduction"—analysed n. 1, 155;
  wartime peak of, 30–1;
  See also Agr., distress of, Corn Laws, Galpin, W. F., Jevons, W. S., Prices, Tooke, T.
Agriculture, progress of:
  account of, 129;
  as measured by production, 132;
  by 1850, 167–8;
  "Golden Age" of Eng. Agr., 178;
  lack of, 10;
  not general (1813–37), 136–7;
  preparations for (1837–46), 137;
  See also Agr., depression in, Board of Agr., Caird, J., Porter, G. R., Young, A.
Agriculture, relief of:
  analysis of proposals for, 172–6;
  Committees on, 101–6, 109–12, 126;
  Corn Laws, 59–63;

Agriculture, relief of:
 in (1821), 105-12, (1836) 136;
 legislation for (1816), 79-86;
 measures proposed (1816), 76-7;
 merits of proposals for, 106-08;
 reduction in National taxes, 134;
 Western's scheme for (1822), 118-19;
 See also Agr., prices, Poor Laws, Tax reduction, Tithe Commutation, Wars
Agriculture, revolution in:
 as supply factor, 144;
 causes of, 8;
 See also Agr., population of, Agr., progress of, Board of Agr., Young, A.
Annals of Agriculture, 11;
 See Young, A.
Anti-Corn Law League:
 formation and success of, 138;
 See also Corn Laws

Bank of England:
 circulation of examined, 160;
 inflationary activities of, 145;
 investigation of (1819), 92;
 notes of redeemed (1825), 122;

Bank of England:
 precarious situation of (1825-6), 121;
 resumption of cash payments by, 94;
 small notes retired by, 136;
 suspension of cash payments by, 27;
 volume of notes outstanding (1815-25), 96;
 See also Bank Restriction Act, Country Banks, Currency, Peel's Bill
Bank Restriction Act:
 Committees on, 92-5;
 passage of, 27;
 termination of, 94;
 See also Bank of England, Gold Standard, inflation, Peel's Bill
Banks. See Bank of England, Country Banks
Baring, Mr., 61, 100
Birch, Wyrley, 77-8
Board of Agriculture:
 activities of, 11;
 data of on agr. distress (1814-16), 70-9;
 data of on farming expense, 35;
 establishment of, 10-11;
 report of on corn trade, 41;
 See also Agr., distress of Agr., progress of, Young, A.
Bounties. See Export Counties, Import Counties

Bowker, Miles, 78
Bright, John, 138
Brougham, Mr., 83, 88
Burdett, Sir Francis, 119
Business depression :
  causes of (1814–16), 65–9 ;
  end of, 104 ;
  recurrence of, 90 ;
  result of crash of 1825–6, 120–2 ;
  See also Agr., depression in, Prices, Wars

Caird, James :
  on agr., 167–8 ;
  See also Agr. progress
Castlereagh, Lord, 85
Cobden, Richard, 138
Coke, Mr., 9
Committees. See Commons, House of
Commons, House of :
  bills on enclosing, 14–15 ;
  Committee on Agr. distress (1820), 99, (1821) 102–3, (1822) 108–9, (1833) 126–7, (1836) 135 ;
  Committee on Bank Restriction Act, 92–5 ;
  Committee on Corn Laws, 57 ;
  Committee on corn trade of Ireland, 39 ;
  Committee on grain trade of United Kingdom, 39–44 ;

Commons, House of :
  Committee on import duties, etc., 84–5 ;
  Committee on Poor Laws, 132 ;
  relief measures defeated in, 111 ;
  remarks on report of Committee (1833), 129–32 ;
  See also Agr., distress of, Legislative relief, Politics
Competition :
  among tenants, 32 ;
  beneficial effects of asserted, n. 1, 171
  foreign, see Corn Laws,
  harmful effects of, 139 ;
  See also Agr., progress of, Agr., prices, Rents, Wages
Continental System :
  abandonment of, 25 ;
  effects of, 23–4 ;
  See also Agr., prices, Foreign trade, Napoleon, Wars
Corn Laws :
  agitation for change in, 91 ;
  as part of Mercantilism, 16 ;
  battle of, 47 ff. ;
  beneficial effects of, 171 ;
  Bill of 1815, 37 ff. ;
  change in proposed, 38–9, 111 ;
  efficacy of, 105 ;

INDEX

Corn Laws:
  history of, 16-20;
  ineffectiveness of, 144;
  petitions against change in, 56-7, 62;
  prices and duties in, n. 2, 20;
  repeal of, 138;
  report of Committees on, 42-4;
  revision of, 138;
  Robinson's resolutions on, 59;
  vote on, 63;
  See also Agr., distress of, Agr., relief of, Agr., prices, Anti-Corn Law League, Foreign trade
Cost of production. See Farming expense
Couling, Mr., 3
Country Banks:
  effects of failure of analysed, n. 1, 154;
  expansion in notes of, 121;
  failure of, 69;
  growth of, 28;
  inflationary activities of, 145;
  notes of, 28-9;
  redeemability of notes deferred, 119-20;
  regulations of revised, 122;
  See also Bank of England, Currency, Peel's Bill, Prices

Crops:
  relative importance of, 4;
  See also Seasons
Currency:
  as demand factor, 144;
  change in laws regulating, 119-20;
  change in vol. of, 96;
  Committee on Bank of England, 92-5;
  Country bank notes, 28-9;
  depreciation of, 145;
  expansion of (1822-5), 121-2;
  legality of, 27;
  regulation of, 95;
  state of, 27-8;
  system reorganised, 122;
  See also Bank of England, Bank Restriction Act, Inflation, Peel's Bill, Prices
Curtler, W. H. R., 175
Curwen, Mr., 82

Deflation:
  as cause of depression, 67-9, 114-18;
  by country banks, n. 1, 154;
  See also Agr., distress of, Bank of England, Country Banks, Peel's Bill
Depression:
  See Agr., depression in, Business depression

Duties:
  effect of on prices, 144;
  method of calculating, n. 2, 18;
  See also Corn Laws, Mercantilism

Embargo Act, 26
Enclosures:
  Bills passed on, 15;
  Committee on, 14;
  need for, 13;
  See also Agr., progress of, Farm lands
English farming about 1800, 1–20
Ernle, Lord, 10
Expenses of farmers:
  complaint about, 74–6;
  during Wars, 35;
  increase in, 148;
  See also Poor Laws, Prices, Rents, Taxes, Tithes, Wages
Export bounty:
  abolition of advocated, 43;
  history of, 16–20;
  restoration of suggested, 81;
  See also Agr., relief of, Corn Laws

Farm depression. See Agr., depression in Agr., distress of
Farm lands:
  amount of, 3;
  distribution of, 3;

Farm lands:
  effect of depression on, 115–16, 127;
  increase in tillage of (1814–33), 130–1;
  See also Agr., distress of, Agr. industries of, Rents
Farm relief. See Agr., relief of
Farmers:
  character of, 165;
  lack of initiative of, 177;
  See also Agr., population of, Landlords, Tenants
Farmer's Magazine, The:
  establishment of, 11;
  on agr. distress, 71;
  on agr. relief (1821), 102;
  on Corn Laws, 56;
  See also Agr., distress of, Agr., relief of
Farming Society of Ireland, The:
  on corn trade, 41
Farms:
  effect of depression on, 127;
  need for large, 12;
  size of, 5;
  size of and relative distress on, 176;
  See also Agr., industries of, Agr., progress of, Leases, Tenants, Rents
Foreign exchange:
  rates of (1820–1), 96–7;
  See also Currency, Gold Standard, Peel's Bill

INDEX

Foreign trade :
  effect on agr. of (1850–60), 177 ;
  effect of on prices, 142–3 ;
  expense of in war and peace, 50 ;
  expenses of, 25 ;
  in agr. produce, 21–2 ;
  in grain (1792–1811), 40, (1800–35) 130–1 ;
  obstructions to, 20–6 ;
  with U.S., 25–6 ;
  See also Continental System, Corn Laws, Corn Law repeal, Free trade, Mercantilism

Free trade :
  arguments against, 90 ;
  arguments for, 88 ;
  effects of after 1846, 138–9;
  petitions for (1820), 100 ;
  probable effect on agr. of, 106 ;
  See also Agr., distress of, Corn Laws, Corn Law repeal, Foreign trade

Galpin, W. F., n. 1, 22
George III, " Farmer George," 12
Gold Standard :
  abandonment of, 27 ;
  abandonment of suggested, 119 ;
  return to, 97 ;
  See also Bank Restriction Act, Currency, Peel's Bill, Prices

Henry III, 16
" High farming " :
  preparations for, 136 ;
  See also Agr., depression in, Agr., progress of, Scotland
Huskisson, Mr., 54, 56, 119, 124

Import bounties :
  amount of (1796–1803), 40 ;
  Government payment of, 19
Import duties :
  change in advocated, 43 ;
  on agr. products, *see* Corn Laws
  See also Foreign trade, Free trade
Industrial Revolution :
  as supply factor, 144 ;
  effect on agr., 8, 147 ;
  effect on politics, 37 ;
  See also Agr., progress of, Agr., revolution in, Young, A.
Interest :
  rate of, n. 1, 83 ;
  See also Farmers' expense
Ireland :
  agr. distress in, 127 ;
  crops of, 4 ;
  landlords of and Corn Laws, 38 ff. ;
  live stock in, 5 ;
  trade with England, 38–41 ;

Ireland:
  treatment under Corn Laws, 17;
  See also Agr., distress of, Agr., prices, Foreign trade

Jevons, W. S., 31, 96, 120, 152, 161, 173

Labourers, Industrial:
  condition of (1819), 91;
  rioting among (1826), 122;
  wages of (1821), 108–14;
  See also Agr., labourers in, Wages
Labourers, Agricultural, See Agr., labourers in
Landlords:
  as sources of relief, 136;
  burden borne by, 168;
  carelessness of, 176;
  condition of (1815), 55, (1833) 130;
  distress of (1814–16), 70–9;
  effect of high prices on, 32;
  expenses of, 33–5
  Irish and Corn Laws, 38–9;
  political power of, 37–8;
  prosperity of, 30–6;
  relations with tenants, 6;
  rents of reduced, 127;
  report on condition of, 103–12, 114–15;
  See also Agr., distress of, Agr., progress of, Leases, Politics, Rents

Lands:
  amount of, 2;
  common, 13;
  distribution of, 13;
  effects of distress on, 127;
  See also Agr., industries of, Enclosures, Farms
Leases:
  customary length of (1800), 6;
  date of payment on, 7;
  effect of short on tenants, 168;
  See also Landlords, Tenants
Legislative relief:
  analysed, 168–78;
  denied petitioners (1836), 136;
  futility of, 108, 129
  in 1816, 85–6;
  merits of proposals for, 109–12;
  See also Agr., relief of, Corn Laws, Politics, Taxes
Letters:
  comment on, n. 1 and 2, 71, n. 4, 77;
  on agr. distress, 71–9;
  See also Board of Agriculture
Licensed trade:
  as cost factor, 142;
  during Wars, 23–4;
  See also Continental System, Foreign trade

INDEX

Lords, House of:
  Committee on Bank of England, 92;
  minority protest on Corn Law, 63;
  See also Agr., relief of, Corn Law, Peel's Bill

McAdam, Mr., 15
McCulloch, J. R., 2, 68
Manufacturers:
  compared with farmers, 165–6;
  depressed condition of, 65–9, 90, 120–2;
  See also Business depression, Corn Laws
Marketing:
  orderly, scheme for, n. 1, 172;
  See also Agr., relief of, Corn Laws
Mercantilism:
  attack on, 89;
  legal manifestations of, 15;
  See also Agr., distress of, Corn Laws, Foreign trade, Wages
Middleton, Mr., 3
Money. *See* Currency

Napoleon, 25, 27
  See also Continental System, Wars
Napoleonic Wars, 1, 21, 64, 141
  cost of, 33–4;
  See also Wars

National debt:
  growth of, 33–4;
  methods of reducing, 118–20;
  See also Agr., distress of, Agr. relief of, Taxes
Non-Intercourse Act:
  effect of, 26;
  See also Foreign trade, U.S.
Norfolk System, 4;
  See also Agr., progress of

Open field system:
  defects of, 13;
  See also Enclosures
" Overproduction ":
  analysis of, n. 1, 155;
  See Agr., prices

Palmer, Mr., 15
" Paper blockades ". *See* Continental System
Parnell, Sir Henry, 39, 45, 51, 56;
  See also Landlords
Peace of Amiens, 22, 141
Peace of Paris, 1, 64, 113
Peterloo Massacre, n. 3, 91;
  See also Business depression
Petitions:
  absence of from tenants, 62;
  against Corn Laws, 57;
  against duties on raw materials, 100;
  for agr. relief, 101, 109, 135;

Petitions:
  for free trade, 100;
  for higher duties, 19, 97;
  remedies suggested in (1836), 136;
  See also Agr., distress of, Agr. relief of, Commons, House of, Corn Laws
Peel, Sir Robert, 62
Peel, " Young Mr.", 92, 138
Peel's Bill:
  effects on agr. of, 117;
  effects on currency of, 96;
  origin of, 92;
  passage of, 94;
  See also Agr., distress of, Bank of England,
Philips, Mr., 60
" Political economists " criticised, 52
Politics:
  and Corn Law of 1815, 37 ff.;
  relation to farm relief, 90–1;
  state of, 37;
  summary of relation to agr. relief, 168–9;
  See also Agr., distress of, Agr., relief of, Corn Laws, Legislative relief, Reform Bill of 1832
Poor Laws:
  administration of, 34–5;
  expense of, 74–5;
  revision of, 132, 171;

Poor Laws:
  See also Agr., distress of, Agr., relief of, Taxes
Population:
  as demand factor, 146;
  change in character of, 131;
  growth of in eighteenth century, 9;
  tax per head of, 134;
  See also Agr., population of
Porter, G. R., 129–32
Pound sterling. See Currency, Gold standard
Prices, general:
  effect on protective duties, 144;
  analysis of during Wars, 141–8;
  comparison with pre-War, 155;
  Corn and meat (1780–1860), 31;
  cause of fall in (1814–16), 65–9;
  deflation of, 153–4;
  effect of fall in on agr., 114–15;
  effect of Peel's Bill on, 96;
  effect of Wars on, 27–31;
  fall in (1818–19), 90–1;
  international aspects of, n. 1, 159;
  studies of, n. 2, 29–30;
  trend of wholesale (1790–1850), 29, 88, 90–1, (1852–60) 177;

INDEX

Prices, general:
  See also Agr., distress of, Agr., prices, Bank Restriction Act, Business depression, Peel's Bill

Queen Victoria, 137

Receiver of Corn Returns, 43;
  See also Corn Laws
Reform Bill of 1832:
  political effect of, 125;
  See also Agr., relief of
Relief. *See* Agr., relief of
Rents:
  during Wars, 32–3;
  effect of high on landlords, 32;
  effect of agr. distress on, 104;
  increase in (1790–1833), 130;
  relative movements in, 167–8;
  See also Agr., distress of, Agr., relief of Leases
Ricardo, David, n. 2, 94, 111, 118;
  on regulation of country bank notes, n. 3, 95;
  opposition of to Govt. purchase of grain, n. 1, 111;
  See also Agr., distress of, Agr., relief of, Commons, House of
Robinson, Frederick, 59, 85, 90, 97, 101

Rose, Mr., 49
"Rotten boroughs." *See* Reform Bill of 1832
Royal Agricultural Society, The, 137

Scotland:
  agr. distress in, 127;
  agr. progress in, 175–6;
  crops of, 4;
  See also Agr., depression of, Agr., relief of, Farmers, Tithes
Seasons:
  as cause of distress (1833–6), 135;
  effect on politics of, 48:
  nature of (1793–1815), 26–7;
  unusually good, 103;
  See also Agr., distress of Agr., prices
Silberling, N. J., 96, 120, 121, 143, 152
Sinclair, Sir John, 11
Standard of living:
  of agr. labourers (1833), 129;
  of tenants and landlords, 55, 147–8, 163;
  See also Agr., distress of, Farming expense, Wages

Tariff. *See* Corn Laws
Taxes:
  Commons committee on, 107;

Taxes:
  local, 34;
  methods of reducing, 119–20;
  national, reduction of, 81–6;
  report on (1833), 126;
  rise of, 33–5;
  sums spent for poor relief (1803–40), 133;
  See also Agr., relief of, Poor Laws, Tithes, Wars
Telford, Mr., 15
Tenants:
  benefits from Tithe Commutation Act, 134;
  competition among, 32;
  condition of (1814) 55, (1821) 102–12, 114–18, (1833) 126, (1836) 136
  distress of (1814–16), 70–9;
  expense of, 33;
  prosperity of, 30–6;
  relations with landlords, 6;
  self-help of, 128;
  See also Agr., distress of, Agr., relief of, Farmers' expenses, Leases, Poor Laws
Tithes:
  amount of, 35;
  Commutation Act, 133–4, 172;
  complaint about, 75–6;
  See also Agr., distress of, Agr., relief of

Tooke, Thomas, 67, 96, 117
Tory Party, 37, 101, 125
  See also Agr., relief of, Corn Laws, Commons, House of, Politics, Reform Bill of 1832
Trade. *See* Foreign trade, Free trade
Turner, B. B., 28

United States:
  depression in (1816–19), 91;
  financial policy of, 159;
  trade with England (1800–14), 25–6;
  See also Foreign trade, Wars

Vansittart, Mr., 79

Wages:
  in agr. depression, 114, 128;
  of agr. and mfg. labourers, 168;
  under Mercantilism, 15;
  See also Agr., labourers in, Agr., distress of, Business depression, Farmers' expense
Wales:
  acreage of with England, 2;
  population of, 7
Warehousing system:
  origin of, 18;

Warehousing system:
  revision of, 123;
  See also Corn Laws
Wars:
  Civil, 139;
  cost of, 33-4;
  Crimean, 139;
  Napoleonic, 21, 64, 141
Western, Mr., 80, 118, 119

Whig Party, 37, 83, 126

Young, Arthur, 3, 5, 12, 13;
  Annals of Agr., editor of, 11;
  Board of Agr., 11;
  success of programme of, 31-2

For Product Safety Concerns and Information please contact our EU representative GPSR@taylorandfrancis.com
Taylor & Francis Verlag GmbH, Kaufingerstraße 24, 80331 München, Germany